PICKETS AT THE GATES

Pickets at the Gates

Estelle Fuchs

THE FREE PRESS, New York
Collier-Macmillan Limited, London

The original studies, "Pickets at the Gates" and "School Boycott," were sponsored by a training grant from the Office of Juvenile Delinquency and Youth Development, Welfare Administration, U. S. Department of Health, Education and Welfare, in cooperation with the President's Committee on Juvenile Delinquency and Youth Crime and with the Department of Education, Hunter College, City University of New York.

PREFACE

IN RECENT YEARS, school personnel have found themselves catapulted into the midst of the most urgent social and economic problems facing the nation. One of these significant issues, the Negro's demand for full integration into American life, has extended from campaigns for civil rights and economic opportunity to pressures upon schools that cannot be ignored. School personnel are finding themselves squarely in the midst of the battleground on which these issues are being fought, for education is often viewed as providing or withholding the key to equality.

That educational equality is essential to equality of opportunity in this country is widely accepted. Yet the massive failure of youngsters in inner-city schools—sometimes known as "ghetto" schools, "slum" schools, "difficult" schools or *de facto* segregated schools—continues to trouble educators and civil rights advocates alike. Often each group places blame on the other. Clashes between school personnel, who consider themselves well meaning in efforts to improve education, and those who view the schools as deliberately withholding opportunities are not infrequent.

All those concerned with the preparation of teachers and administrators who will be working with the populations of the inner city recognize the need to develop improved understanding of these disagreements. *Pickets at the Gates* is one effort aimed at providing instructional material that utilizes social-science concepts to illuminate current educational problems. The materials were designed for use in the preservice and in-service education of teachers and administrators. They have applicability as well to all those concerned with human relations and integration.

Pickets at the Gates was originally prepared under the auspices of Project TRUE, or Teachers and Resources for Urban Education. Project TRUE is sponsored by Grant Numbers 64227 and 65230, Office of Juvenile Delinquency and Youth Development, United States Department of Health, Education and Welfare, and by the Department of Education, Hunter College, City University of New York.

The author is indebted to Dr. Marjorie B. Smiley, Director of Project TRUE for her careful and constructive reading of the manuscript. Dr. Elizabeth M. Eddy, Director of Research, Project TRUE; Dr. Paula Rubel; Dr. Eleanor Leacock; Dr. Mary Owen Cameron; and Professors Helen Storen and Ronald O. Doll gave generously of their time to read and comment on various portions of the book.

In Part Two, the interviews with children that form a large portion of the text were conducted by Mrs. Helen Randolph, a member of the Project TRUE staff. Her skill and empathy were responsible for creating excellent interview conditions, and her contributions to this study proved invaluable.

Miss Elaine Paul, Mrs. Masako Mae Kanazawa, and Mr. Norman Bailey, typists, rendered gracious assistance, as did

Miss Carol Gibbons, Miss Carol Bryant, Mrs. Susan Stein, and Miss Evelyn McVeigh.

Special thanks go to all the public-school personnel, freedom-school staff, children, civil-rights leaders, and the many others who contributed their time and perceptions to this examination of problems posed by school boycotts. Despite disagreement and varying interpretations concerning cause and effect, all evinced great concern for improving the education of the children of the city. All seek greater understanding of the myriad problems involved and co-operated fully.

Finally, I am profoundly indebted to my husband, Willy, who has been a knowledgeable critic and patient supporter throughout the preparation of this work.

Estelle Fuchs

CONTENTS

PART ONE

PICKETS AT THE GATES

INTRODUCTION

THIS IS THE STORY of how one school principal found himself, quite unexpectedly, in the heart of the Negro's struggle for full equality. It is based upon an event that occurred in a large metropolitan area. The incident vividly illustrates many of the problems facing school personnel today. The problems concern the significance of administrators' attitudes toward their role and that of the school toward children, teachers, parents. They also concern school-community relations in a period of rapid social change.

Data for the case were gathered from a series of interviews with persons directly involved in the events: The principal and his assistants, several teachers, other principals, the president of the parents' organization, other parents, the manager of a local housing development, several ministers, representatives from the Board of Education, the leader of a civil-rights organization, and the local press were consulted for information. Names and some details were altered in order to protect the identities of the informants.

Pickets at the Gates was not intended to be a community study. We have sought only to examine the relative forces operating in this case in the light of social science concepts. School personnel are being asked to help solve some of the most pressing social problems of our day. If, hopefully, we achieve heightened awareness and understanding of their involvement, we shall have accomplished our aim.

The following material falls into three chapters. The first describes the event; the second explores relevant factors needed to ensure fruitful discussion. A discussion and comment by the author form the third chapter. Where this case is used as classroom material, we believe that it may be useful for discussion and comment to be made by students before proceeding to Chapter 3. Therefore, questions for discussion have been included following Chapter 2.

1. THE EVENT

PICKETS AT THE GATES, petitions demanding his dismissal, articles about him in a large metropolitan newspaper—never in his fourteen years at Samuel Slater School had Mr. Fields, the principal, faced such an unpleasant situation. Could this have happened because of the letter he sent his teachers? All he had done, he thought, was to attempt some meaningful teacher orientation. Instead, he engendered the enmity of many of the parents. What had caused such a commotion?

The Samuel Slater Elementary School is located in an area of *de facto* segregation in a large northern metropolitan city. Because of the residential patterns, 71 per cent of the school population is Negro, the remainder almost all Puerto Rican. Mr. Fields, the principal, had worked in this area for fourteen years. Each year he had faced the problem of teacher turnover. This year fifteen new, inexperienced teachers, recently graduated from college, had been assigned to the school. A man in late middle age, with grown children of his own, Mr. Fields prided himself on his fatherly approach to the new teachers. Increasingly he had become aware of the need to help them toward a better understanding of the children with whom they would be working and the community in which they would be working.

Mr. Fields anticipated that, with rare exceptions, his new teachers would be young white women who had had very little, if any, firsthand acquaintance with conditions in a Negro and Puerto Rican neighborhood. Their student-teaching experience would probably not have included working in a school of this population, and, even if it had, such experience was widely known to be a sheltered, relatively artificial one. He believed, because of past experience, that many of the new teachers had grown up in middle-class white communities and had little acquaintance with people outside their families and college friends. He assumed that many had never been exposed to poverty or the breakdown of family to be found in the community to which they had now been assigned.

This year he had been reading a great deal concerning the characteristics of children in depressed areas. Finding the materials very interesting, he felt that they would be of value to his teachers. Thus, in an effort to cushion the shock he felt the young teachers might suffer upon meeting the children of this community, he sent the following letter to his faculty:

Welcome back from vacation time. I hope that you have recharged your batteries and are ready for the challenges of the coming academic year.

Some of you are younger and more spirited than your older colleagues. It is to you that this letter is primarily addressed. Your more experienced colleagues can corroborate what follows:

Our school receives many special services such as smaller registers, more money per child, and teacher specialists. Why do we get these special services?

Our children, for the most part, come from homes that are usually disadvantaged. That means that, compared with middle class homes, they are poorer financially, academically, socially. Specifically, many of our children are on welfare. We serve over 500 free lunches daily. The school lunch is the best meal they get.

Many of our children have no father at home. There can be no organized family activities. There is lacking a male image. The mother is so busy with her brood that the individual child is lonely. He has no conversation with the mother or other adults. He is unaccustomed to listen. In fact, living in a noisy atmosphere, he has a high hearing level, i.e., he shuts out most noises and sounds in self-protection. Hence he is not going to hear his middle class teacher who speaks quietly, until he has been trained to do so by his teacher who has this as one of her conscious, specific aims.

The language he hears at home may be Spanish. Or, it may be the poor speech of a parent who is illiterate or of limited schooling. The Spanish child knows that his parent does not speak English so he is more likely to imitate his teacher's speech. The other child acts on the assumption that his parent speaks English and hence is less likely, possibly, to imitate the teacher. An intense attention to correct speech by your children is most essential.

Furthermore, there is lack of encouragement at home to achieve. There may be absent adequate male models. Families on welfare for the third generation lack academic drive.

The physical situation at home may be deplorable. Cold flats, no hot water, peeling paint and falling plaster, vermin, overcrowding—these are the characteristics of the homes of some of our children. For such children, school is an oasis from squalor. You will find that your attendance is highest on the coldest days, for school is clean and warm.

Coming from a poor environment, socially, culturally, economically, physically, it is no wonder that our children are not ready for school when they enter and that, in the case of some of them, there is a cumulative decline in academic achievement as they move along in a school whose staff is middle class and whose values confuse some of the children. Specifically the proper care of textbooks, the keeping of an accurate, neat, complete notebook, punctuality, proper dress and cleanliness are things which we have to teach the children, and, unfortunately, some parents. These are characteristics of poverty irrespective of ethnic groups. The people of the Appalachian Mountains, the Ozark hill-billies, the Mexican-American migrant farm workers, have these attributes as well as poor Negroes and poor Puerto Ricans.

One purpose of this letter is to help you rid yourself of certain misconceptions: not "all slum children are slow learners." Actually, "underprivileged kids have just as wide a range of abilities as middle class kids." (Prof. A. Harry Passow at Teachers College) Hence, you must not have the idea that your role is chiefly custodial—that if you keep them quiet and in their seats you have earned your salary; you haven't. Mere custodians are taking their checks under false pretenses. You have a license as a teacher. That is your job—to teach—to teach with all these difficulties in mind, to try to compensate for their handicaps. If you are indifferent to their academic achievement or lack of it, they will continue to be indifferent, for their poor environment and minority group status are not their fault. Nor is it yours. But it *is* your responsibility to plan your work with these facts in mind.

What are you going to have as your basic goals? Of primary importance is social living. Unless your class has real discipline, not authoritarian order, you don't have a real teaching-learning situation. We line the children up quietly. They go into the building quietly; they go to your room quietly. Then, it's up to you.

Your first days will be devoted to training in routine; mechanical aspects of the classroom must be mechanized. You will see to it that the children are clean, that every child's hair is combed, and that every boy has a necktie on.

There are certain basic academic skills that you will stress. These are:

1. Listening
2. Reading
3. Expression of ideas
4. Mathematics

Your "School Manual" has specific suggestions for these and other areas. Read it. Consult it. Don't let it gather dust. Use it in preparing at home. It is easier to prepare interesting lessons at home than to fight a disciplinary situation resulting from boredom with an uninteresting lesson.

Through our P.T.A. we are going to try to instill a greater sense of responsibility in some of our parents. We will try to get them to understand the importance of:

1. Cleanliness
2. Proper dress
3. Punctuality
4. Attendance—unless ill
5. Care of school property
6. Neat, clean, complete, accurate notebooks
7. Academic achievement

From you the teachers I expect:

1. Punctuality
2. Careful preparation
3. Functioning on a level above that of the children
4. "Know how to call to the man which has lain dormant within the soul of the child."

There are many other things I could say, but this letter is much too long already. Hence, I shall say no more at this time.

But I do pledge you on behalf of the three supervisors our complete cooperation and aid. Their activities will be not only in the school, but in the community at large too, for there are certain responsibilities that the community must assume and not purge itself of a sense of guilt by criticizing the schools.

Mr. Fields, wishing to let the parents know how the school was helping new teachers do a better job, sent a copy of the letter to the president of the Parent-Teachers' Association.

At the P.T.A. executive board meeting held that week, Mrs. Post, the president, reported the communication from the principal. She was somewhat apprehensive about doing so because she felt the letter had been unwise, and she wished she could have discussed it with Mr. Fields before the meeting. Upon reading the letter, several parent members of the board immediately became infuriated. They viewed the letter as insulting, degrading, and designed to hurt their children. Although the executive board took no official action at this time, largely because of Mrs. Post's urging, discussion of the letter and anger at the principal became the keynote of the entire meeting. An unofficial committee was formed by several executive board members to see the principal and demand an apology.

When the committee called upon him, Mr. Fields was absolutely astonished. Indignant at what he considered an unjustified response by the parents to his sincere efforts to improve the school, he informed the parents that he had intended no harm and saw no need to apologize.

Angered by the principal's refusal to apologize, the parents' committee began to circulate in the neighborhood of the school the following petition calling for his ouster:

On September 11, 1964, Mr. Fields, Principal of Slater School, issued a letter to the school teaching staff in which he made the following comments about our community —our parents—our children:

a. "compared with middle class homes, they are poorer financially, academically, socially."
b. "many of our children are on welfare . . . the school lunch is the best meal they get."

c. "the mother is so busy with her brood that the individual child is lonely."
d. "many of our children have no father at home."
e. Our children are "living in a noisy atmosphere."
f. "there is a lack of encouragement at home to achieve."
g. "Families on welfare for the third generation lack academic drive."
h. "Coming from a poor environment, socially, culturally, economically, physically, it is no wonder that our children are not ready for school . . ."
i. "the people of the Appalachian Mountains, the Ozark hill-billies, the Mexican-American migrant workers, have these attributes as well as poor Negroes and poor Puerto Ricans."

Do these comments accurately describe you and your family? We deplore these intemperate, injudicious and uninformed remarks. They speak more to the discredit of Mr. Fields than any of our families. We contend that these remarks represent Mr. Fields' attitude toward us and our children. The image he presents is insulting, inaccurate and detrimental. No school can thrive under this caliber of leadership. Indeed, Mr. Fields refused, when asked by parents, to apologize.

We, the undersigned, demand the removal of Mr. Fields from the principalship of Slater School.

In addition to circulating the petition, the protesting parents contacted the leaders of a militant, citywide organization working for rapid school integration in order to inform them of the incidents. Soon the events at Slater were reported in a newspaper having a large circulation among Negroes in the city:

Parents Demand Principal's Ouster For Remark

Negro parents Tuesday circulated a petition demanding the removal of Mr. Fields, principal of the Samuel Slater Elementary School, following his refusal to apologize for comments about Negro children and their families which the parents considered "intemperate, injudicious, and un-informed . . ."

The newspaper article contained excerpts from Mr. Fields' letter and concluded with a quotation from a leader of the organization contacted by the parents:

> . . . "This letter is the kind of ignorant attitude that the Negro community will no longer tolerate. It dramatizes the need for more Negroes in supervisory positions in the school system."

One afternoon, several pickets appeared before the gates of the Slater School. They carried placards which read, "MR. FIELDS MUST GO, HE IS ANTI-NEGRO."

Mr. Fields was shocked by the turn of events. He had served the Slater area for fourteen years, and had hoped to finish his term until retirement there. His school was bright and cheerful. A new building had replaced one almost one hundred years old just four years ago. He was pleased with his staff, which included two assistants to the principal, teachers he considered dedicated (for, as he said, "hadn't they stayed here rather than seek transfers to middle class white schools"), and newcomers who made up in enthusiasm and energy what they lacked in experience. And now, this!

Upon learning of the petition calling for his dismissal, Mr. Fields contacted the assistant superintendent in charge of the school district in which Slater was located. The principal explained that his intention in giving the letter to his teachers was to provide them with guidance concerning the school situation in which they would be working. The assistant superintendent in turn notified the division that had been established by the Board of Education to deal with problems arising between community and school, particularly problems involving school integration. A meeting among the parents, the principal, the representative from the Board of Education, and the assistant superintendent was arranged.

Fully expecting the representative from the Board of Education and the assistant superintendent to agree with him that the parents had been unjustified and unfair in their criticism, Mr. Fields found that the Board of Education people did not agree with him. At this meeting they were especially concerned that the parents' objections to the letter be aired. The president of the P.T.A. spoke, explaining that the major objections were concerned with what the parents felt to be an erroneous impression and description of the school. She explained that the parents feared that these impressions would affect the way in which their children would be treated and taught, for the parents were anxious that their children not be given inferior schooling.

Mr. Fields continued to maintain that inferior education was not his aim at all, nor did he intend to offend the parents. The representative from the Board of Education urged Mr. Fields to apologize if he were asked again.

The following week an open P.T.A. meeting was held at the school. The main item on the agenda was a report on the special reading program of the school. The discussion was led by one of Mr. Fields' assistants. The principal was present, anticipating floor discussion concerning himself. Representatives from the Board of Education and the district superintendent's office were there also. However, the issues concerning the petition and the apology were not raised. Instead, many questions were asked by parents about the curriculum of the Slater School, and several parents wanted to know why Slater should have services and programs any different from schools in more advantaged sections of the city. They saw these differences as indicating that the other schools were better. The assistant principal and the representative of the superintendent of the district explained that any differences which existed at Slater were designed to improve the education of the children. It was clear, however, that many in the audience felt that segregated schooling in the area was inferior.

In an effort to repair the strained relations with the parents, Mr. Fields invited Mrs. Post, the president of the P.T.A., to speak to his faculty. She declined his invitation, but did agree to write a statement the principal sent to all members of the staff. In this letter Mrs. Post wrote:

> The children of the Slater area come from a wide variety of backgrounds . . . The teacher can function in this particular area best by teaching the children to function beyond any social or economic handicaps they may bring to school.

The issues of the petition and the apology were not raised again. Mr. Fields recognized that he had done something unwise—he certainly would be more careful about what he put on paper in the future—but he still could see nothing terribly wrong in what he wrote. He considered the parents to be hypersensitive, and he believed their criticism of him to be unwarranted and unfair. He was cheered somewhat by a letter to the editor which appeared in the newspaper which had reported the parents' protest:

> Dear Editor:
> I read with some concern the complaint that has been lodged against the principal of Slater School, Mr. Fields. I am a Negro mother who has children in the public school system. I happen also to be a teacher who works in the same district where the Slater School is located.
> Therefore, I can say authoritatively that if I lived in this district, I would not hesitate to send my children to the Slater School for the following reasons: Mr. Fields runs a well organized school, he has a very stable staff

and Mr. Fields exerts every possible means to keep academic standards high.

I know Mr. Fields. I know the area. I can honestly say that Mr. Fields' letter has been unfortunately misinterpreted. I do not believe he had any intention of insulting the Negro population, but rather, he desired to create an awareness of some problems which do exist in the community that could possibly prevent the students from performing to the maximum of their potential.

I am distressed that the communication between the principal and the community that surrounds the school could have deteriorated to this state. I only hope that an attempt be made to create a more amicable atmosphere in the interest of the children.

MRS. JANE RICHARDSON

News of the Slater situation was widely discussed by other principals throughout the city, for they were concerned that one of their colleagues had been involved in such conflict. Several feared the possibility of similar events occurring to them. Mr. Fields had a reputation for being a forthright, liberal person, very egalitarian in his outlook, and for him to be accused of bigotry and intolerance seemed quite surprising.

Many of his colleagues had faced similar situations. Several had had their schools boycotted, and they expected further boycotts to occur. Many were finding themselves accused by civil rights groups of the very things they had rejected all their lives—intolerance and racism, as well as poor educational leadership. It was distressing to them to find themselves accused of the very things they opposed.

Thus, at Slater, a communication from a principal to his staff concerning the children and school goals acquired a significance that reached out beyond the confines of the school to involve parents, the school board, colleagues, political pressure groups, and the press. Why should the contents of Mr. Fields' letter have aroused such controversy and widespread interest? In order to answer this and other questions concerning the forces affecting the functions of the school in the city of today, we must turn to a more detailed examination of the area in which the Slater School is located and to an examination of the school itself.

2. RELEVANT FACTORS

THE NEIGHBORHOOD

THE SLATER SCHOOL is located in a section of the city that has been populated by Negro people for more than two generations. In recent years Puerto Rican families have moved into this area. Until about five years ago the streets were lined with dilapidated housing dating from the last century. The school itself was over ninety years of age.

Five years ago, however, the area began to undergo a marked physical change. Large numbers of streets were cleared of their substandard houses. In their place arose a series of housing developments giving a markedly different aspect to the neighborhood. Where the old school once stood, there is now a playground, and adjacent to it, in place of the decrepit Victorian structure which once was Slater, there now stands a modern, bright, sprawling, two-story building.

The largest of the new housing developments opened its doors to tenants three years ago. It is a low-income municipal housing project called Skyview Terrace Apartments. This development accommodates almost 800 families in apartments ranging in size from three to eight rooms. While planning this development, the housing authority paid careful attention to providing adequate bedroom space for large families. Rentals range up to $100, and income ceilings for tenants go to $6,000.

It is interesting to note that, when apartments first became available, the advertisements issued by the municipal housing authority were almost indistinguishable from those of private housing developers charging rentals two and three times as high. Thus the advertisements included such appeals as:

> Skyview Terrace is located in a pleasant residential community which includes many new buildings. There are co-operatives and luxury apartments nearby. . . .
> Excellent transportation . . .
> Skyview Terrace is close to the heart of the city's cultural center. . . .
> There are many public, private and parochial schools . . .
> Houses of worship for every faith . . .

Attractive floor plans accompanied the advertisements, and the facts of municipal housing and application procedures were discreetly placed at the end of the flyer. The very name of the development conveyed the image of more elegant housing than that ordinarily associated with low-income projects.

Skyview Terrace attracted as tenants a population group composed of 60 percent Negroes, 20 per cent Puerto Ricans, and 20 per cent others. Most of the white children attend the local parochial schools, whereas most of the Negro and Puerto Rican children attend the Slater School, making up

45 per cent of that school's population. Many of the long-time residents of the community chose to live in Skyview Terrace, impressed with its obvious advantages. Several reported they chose to stay because of their attachment to local churches. Others pointed to convenient transportation to work. Skyview Terrace also contained many families who had moved into the apartments from different sections of the city. Some families came from the suburbs. Combined with the new school structure, the immediate environs of Slater almost give the physical image of a more advantaged area of the city, the one jarring note being the presence of the old police station.

At the time of selection for apartments, each family included a husband and wife with children. Although a few of the families have since broken up, the vast majority of the homes have remained intact.

The majority of the men in the project are semiskilled and skilled workmen. Many are at the factory-foreman level; some are truck drivers, diemakers, radio, TV, and electronics workers. Some are civil-service employees, including postal workers and policemen, and some are teachers at lower salary levels.

Several of the tenants are very articulate, and in the project they have maintained two newspapers, have conducted recreational activities, and have begun to organize a preschool kindergarten. When the parents first began discussions concerning the preschool classes, they inquired as to whether or not the Board of Education, which at that time was developing a program of preschool training for children, would act as sponsor. They made it clear, however, that they wished no program designed for "deprived" or depressed-area children. The Board did not provide a school, and the parents proceeded to organize and staff a voluntary play group themselves.

Although there has not been a great deal of turnover, when

white families leave the development they tend to be replaced by Negroes. Thus living in Skyview Terrace has not
represented escape from the residential ghetto.

It appears that the tenants view Skyview Terrace as the
place where they expect to stay and raise their families,
most of the children attending the Slater School. The manager of the development reported that several families
whose income had risen above the ceiling requested permission to remain. Thus far management has taken a liberal
view and permitted this. Many tenants have furnished
their apartments attractively (several of the apartments
had been furnished as models by local department stores)
and have grown very attached to them. It would be ex-
traordinarily difficult to duplicate the housing at these rentals. One woman said, "Where could we find such nice
apartments at this rent?" Despite all this, a concern over
the school segregation resulting from the residential-
ghetto environment has remained with many.

Annual checks by the housing management have found
that, on the whole, incomes of the people in the development
are rising. However, illness and seasonal unemployment
have created serious financial problems for some who have
been unable to meet the rental payments. In such situations, management refers the cases for welfare services
to help tide the people over the periods of emergency. A
large industry located nearby is expected to leave the city
shortly. This is likely to cause major problems for many
of the residents employed by that industry.

The tenants avoid welfare as long as they can. Several
Puerto Rican families have returned to Puerto Rico when
faced with employment problems. Other families have
moved in with relatives. To go on welfare, for the residents
of this development, represents failure and loss of status.
It is avoided as much as possible. Most of the welfare clients
who live here are dependent children or elderly people.

Beyond the housing-project area stretch many streets containing privately owned multiple-dwelling buildings, as well as one- and two-family homes. Some of the smaller homes are occupied by Negro doctors, lawyers, clergymen, and other professionals. A few send their children to Slater. Many send their children to private schools.

Most of the residents of the neighborhood are not professionals. The men earn their livings as hospital workers, porters, and chauffeurs and in factory work and civil service. Many women work too, earning their livings as domestics, hospital workers, laundry workers, phone operators, civil servants, and saleswomen.

The area of older dwellings, which provides Slater with almost 55 per cent of its pupil population, contains people who have lived there for several generations. It also contains some newcomers from the rural South, as well as recent migrants from Puerto Rico, a relatively new population group in this area that has been predominantly Negro for many years. Several large churches are nearby, and many political clubs, small church sects, and professional and business clubs dot the area.

Because of their relative absence of industrial job skills and a history of discrimination, many of the men who live in this neighborhood find unemployment a constant threat. Several local civic groups have played an active part in demands for the breakdown of discrimination in unions and industrial training programs.

Some of the more economically impoverished children come from streets containing dilapidated rooming houses, which had once been more widespread in this area. These streets are beyond the area of new housing and are not visible from the school. Many of the children who go to Slater come from families who are dependent upon welfare services for their maintenance, and many families not on welfare receive supplementary aid for the children.

Some sociologists have distinguished between the "working-class" and "lower-class" subcultures in America. They describe the former as consisting of stable families headed by males. The "lower-class" subculture, on the other hand, is typified by a female-based family in which the male is present part of the time and is recognized neither as a stable nor as a dominant member of the household.[1] Although the tenements near Slater contain working-class and even "middle-class" families, they also contain many female-based families, and it was this latter group that Mr. Fields viewed as presenting the school with its "problems."

As the advertisements for the Skyview housing development had promised, there are also luxury apartments nearby, and a huge, attractive series of twenty-two-story cooperative apartment buildings is rising behind the Slater School. Over 60 per cent of the people purchasing apartments are Negroes. When the houses are occupied, the children from some of these buildings will be assigned to the school. Whether or not this will represent a shift in the Slater School population remains to be seen. One factor affecting the trend will be the numbers of school-age children who will reside there. Another factor has to do with whether or not these more prosperous families choose to send their children to public school. Already a marked preference for private and parochial schools is evinced among the families who have moved into the completed buildings. Several families have requested permission from the Board of Education to send their children to schools with more integrated populations.

THE SCHOOL

The Slater School draws a population of about 1150 children from this neighborhood. Seventy-one per cent of the

[1] For a summary of this literature see Herbert Gans, *The Urban Villagers: Group and Class in the Life of Italian-Americans* (New York: The Free Press, 1962), pp. 229-262.

pupils are Negroes, 23 per cent are of Puerto Rican background, and 6 per cent represent other groups. Forty-five per cent of the children come from Skyview Terrace, 55 per cent from outside the project. Although, as Mr. Fields was aware, there is a wide range of ability and achievement levels among this population, on the whole the levels of school achievement in standardized mathematics and reading tests fell beneath the citywide norms for the various grades but not significantly lower than those noted in other city schools located in *de facto* segregated areas. The Standardized Achievement Test average scores for the school were

6th Year Reading	4.6
6th Year Mathematics	4.7
3rd Year Reading	2.4
3rd Year Mathematics	2.1

The principal reported that the Skyview Terrace development has led to better attendance, a decline in truancy, decreased pupil transience, improved behavior in school, and greater parental activity.

As indicated, many Slater School children come from families who fall within the lowest socioeconomic levels of the city population. Thus Slater School serves 500 free lunches daily. However, eligibility for a free school lunch does not necessarily mean that a child is being supported by welfare services. In order to be eligible for a free school lunch, a child has to come from a family with a low income, the amount of money determining eligibility varying with the number of children in the family. Thus a family with an employed head and not on welfare can still be eligible for free lunch services for its children. Many Skyview Terrace children receive free lunches, as do children from the older sections of the area. Slater is fortunate in having a modern kitchen, and the lunchroom facilities are cheerful and clean.

As also mentioned, because of the lower levels of achieve-ment and the economic needs of the Slater School popula-tion, the school has been assigned some extra services by the Board of Education. Slater is only one of many schools in the city receiving such services. Class registers have been lowered to thirty. Several special teachers of reading, library services, and guidance have been assigned to the school. Several specialists in the various branches of in-struction pay visits to consult with the teachers on curricu-lum. The staff consists of forty-two teachers, two assistants-to-principal, and the principal.

Mr. Fields has been principal of Slater School for over fourteen years. He has risen through the ranks of the school system, in which he has worked for over thirty years. The son of immigrant parents, he worked hard, studied, and passed through the rigorous licensing procedures to attain the position he now holds. When he was first assigned to the Slater School, in the heart of what was then an all-Negro neighborhood, he anticipated enormous problems, and he was not disappointed. The pupil-transience rate was tre-mendous—there were years when some classes had as high as 80 per cent turnover in pupil population. He also antic-ipated staffing difficulties.

Staffing had been a problem throughout the city, and the situation at Slater was very serious. There were several reasons for this. For a number of years, the growing sub-urbs attracted young teachers, offering them higher sal-aries and newer buildings in which to work. Working in slum areas did not offer high prestige, and teachers either avoided going to them or, of many who did, sought transfers to different schools. Again, many young women assigned to his school left after marriage to raise families. In addition, several older teachers retired. Thus there were periods in the last fourteen years when Slater had a staff turnover of over 50 per cent.

Now there was a new building, city salaries had been raised, and teachers were appointed to schools regardless of their choice. With the teacher shortage waning and job availability no longer so great, there were still fifteen vacancies at Slater in the year in question. Some of these vacancies were filled by newly appointed young teachers who had done their practice teaching here, and the administration of the school was proud that it had achieved improved stability of staff.

Slater School now has a staff of forty-two teachers. Of these, nineteen are permanent teachers with three or more years of experience. Twelve are regularly licensed teachers but have taught less than three years. Eleven of the teachers are substitutes. On the whole, the staff is very young, most of the teachers being in their twenties.

Many of the teachers, young and inexperienced, feel frustrated frequently because they do not find themselves particularly effective in their teaching. Once a week a group of new teachers is relieved from classroom teaching in order to attend a workshop conducted by a group leader sent from the Board of Education. At this workshop, Negro history, Puerto Rican culture, and racial attitudes are discussed. This workshop was established after the controversy over the letter. It is designed to aid in teacher orientation. The leader of the workshop has found many of the teachers to be fairly rigid in their beliefs and has found that it is easier for them to blame lack of academic achievement on the parents or the children rather than on their own inadequacies as teachers.

Over the years, Mr. Fields discovered that he had what he considered to be a certain advantage in this school, which some of his colleagues in other, more advantaged areas of the city did not. For many years he was not under great pressure from the parents or the superintendent concerning the school. His friends who were principals often complained to him about the constant irritations from parents who seemed to know every little thing going on in the school, demanded all kinds of enriched educational programs, and were upset when their children did not get assigned to classes for the gifted. These colleagues complained that too many middle-class parents were either pushing their children or pampering them and demanding of the schools the kind of enriched educational program that a public school finds it difficult to provide. His friends told of those parents who were constantly concerned about teachers' giving their children traumatic experiences. "They're always running up to tell you what Dr. Spock said." At Slater, the problem existed in reverse, as the principal had generally found it difficult to get parents to come to school when teachers wished to discuss their children's difficulties, despite the frequent notes he sent home to parents.

Faced with what he considered the enormous educational, social, and economic problems of his school population, Mr. Fields believed strongly that he had done what he could with a limited staff to run an efficient school. He pointed with pride to his success in maintaining an orderly environment at Slater. He earned the praise of his superintendent for his efforts. Among his colleagues he developed a reputation for being a "dedicated principal." The years slipped by quickly, and, becoming comfortable in this situation, Mr. Fields chose to remain in this school when the opportunity to transfer did arise.

As principal of the school, he had frequent opportunities to address meetings of leaders concerned with affairs in the several neighborhoods around the Slater area. He made constant approaches to them to encourage parental interest in school affairs and to arouse concern for pupil achievement. Never did he admit to any inadequacy on the part of Slater in this regard. To him this was as good a school as any to be found in the city insofar as its leadership, facilities, and program were concerned. If there were in-

adequacies in achievement, Mr. Fields believed they were
to be explained in terms of irresponsibility on the part of
parents who did not appear when summoned to school to
participate in discussions concerning their children's difficulties and also by what he believed to be the inadequate
preparation of the children for the school experience. Mr.
Fields firmly held that there was no reason why a willing
child, with parents who supported the school's efforts,
couldn't be as well educated in this school as in any in the
city, despite *de facto* segregation.

THE PARENTS

During the past three years a marked change in attitude
toward the school has arisen. The articulate members of
the Skyview Terrace development have become active in
the P.T.A. In addition, a segment of the Negro and Puerto
Rican community throughout the city has vociferously attacked the existence of *de facto* segregated schools and has
opposed the view that such schools can be effective. Northern *de facto* segregation has been attacked by spokesmen
for the integration movement in ways similar to the point
of view expressed by Whitney Young, Executive Director of
the National Urban League, who writes:

> Efforts at achieving racially balanced public schools are
> often as heatedly contested in the North as in the South.
> Spokesmen for the anti-integration groups usually claim
> the "neighborhood school" is the ultimate in educational
> wisdom, if it is not divinely inspired. They deplore "ar-
> tificial" solutions, such as busing, redrawing district lines,
> pairing under the Princeton Plan, educational parks or lo-
> cating new schools just outside the ghetto.
> Presumably, it has not occurred to these groups that
> the existing racial segregation is a vicious artificiality. All-
> white neighborhoods and schools didn't just happen. It
> took "genius" and conscious and deliberate planning to

gerrymander them into being and genius is now required to undo this mischief.

Negro children have inherited the oldest, worst, and most rundown school plants in our big cities; supplied with the shoddiest and oldest texts; and are being instructed by the least qualified teachers available—generally substitutes uncertified, or temporary instructors—with some rare and magnificent exceptions.

One result is the widespread notion among white parents that Negro children are slow learners, when, in fact, anthropologists and scientists can find no significant intellectual or mental difference between the races.

The high drop out rates in Negro high schools, therefore, are in large measure a testimony to the failure of the "don't care" attitude of school boards in consciously or unconsciously writing off the potential of Negro children. A comparison of the amount spent for their schooling as compared to white children tends to substantiate the prevalence of this attitude.[2]

Principals often defend the educational programs offered in their *de facto* segregated schools by pointing to new buildings and increased educational services provided for the children in recent years. To these arguments, Professor Kenneth B. Clark answers that the kind of problem faced by children in segregated schools in the North ". . . indicates that they are no longer primarily the problems of flagrant racial discrimination, inferior physical facilities, gerrymandering of school-district lines, and other forms of overt exclusion of Negro children from the academic and specilized levels of education." More significant than these factors, argues Professor Clark, is that

Specifically, these contemporary problems inherent in segregated education involve the degree to which stereo-

<hr>

[2] Whitney Young, "Education and Artificiality," *Amsterdam News*, September 19, 1964.

typed assumptions concerning the inferiority or limited intellectual potentialities of large groups of children lead to the lowering of educational standards in the schools which they are required to attend, the degree to which these conditions, in fact, depress the educational aspirations and level of performance of these children thereby permanently impairing their ability to learn.[3]

In response to the pressures for greater school integration, children from *de facto* segregated schools have been permitted by the Board of Education to register in schools in other areas of the city. Practically none of the parents in the Slater area has chosen to transfer children, preferring that they stay nearer home. However, the parents have become increasingly critical and watchful over the school.

Before Skyview Terrace had been built, the parents of this neighborhood had very little contact with the teachers or the administration, avoiding summonses to school to discuss problems. On parents' visiting day perhaps two or three would show up. The president of the P.T.A. and the assistant principal both reported that this year, after all the excitement concerning the letter, 85 to 100 per cent of the parents came to school on visiting day, indicating a concerned parent body. The militant Negro residents of Skyview were the leaders of the parents. Whereas he once faced a parent body characterized by apparent apathy and avoidance of the school, now Mr. Fields is faced with a parent body that is so concerned with what goes on that a communication from himself to his teachers provoked widespread discussion and the call for his dismissal.

Slater is hardly the peaceful place it used to be for Mr. Fields, as far as relations with parents are concerned. He was quite unprepared for the parents' reaction to what he considered a valid presentation to his beginning teachers.

[3] Kenneth B. Clark, "Segregated Schools in New York City," *Journal of Educational Sociology*, February 1963, p. 249.

Although as an interested citizen he could not escape being aware of the widespread growing interest in school affairs indicated by civil-rights groups in the city, he was taken aback at a direct attack on him, not only for what he believed to be a sound point of view, but also for what he believed to be an intraschool concern between himself and his teachers.

QUESTIONS FOR DISCUSSION

1. Why did the letter offend some of the parents? How could the principal have oriented his teachers without antagonizing the parents?

2. What changes have been occurring in the Slater area that explain the increased parental interest in school affairs that has developed in recent years? Why is it difficult, sometimes, to get parents to school to discuss the difficulties their children are having?

3. Do you believe it is possible to have high academic achievement in a school populated mainly by Negro and/or Puerto Rican children? Explain.

4. What would be the implications of a feeling of negativism on the part of the teachers in this school? How could the principal have avoided presenting a negative picture of the school population?

5. Why is it that language useful to professionals is sometimes resented by laymen?

6. What evidence is there to indicate a conflict between the functions of the school as outlined by the principal and the functions of the school as viewed by the parents?

7. In what ways did the letter reflect the principal's value system?

8. Describe the various groups with which a school principal must maintain relationships. What are the possible conflicts between the demands of these groups that place strain upon the principal? How can the resultant tensions be reduced?

9. Describe and discuss procedures that can be taken to establish constructive school-community relations.

10. What additional information would you like to have to enable you to discuss each of these questions with greater assurance? Explain the relevance of each kind of information you would like to have.

3. DISCUSSION AND COMMENT

ALTHOUGH THERE IS no simple answer as to why conflict occurred at Slater, a careful examination of the events points to three major considerations that may increase our perceptions. These include an incomplete understanding on the part of the principal concerning the social forces at work within the neighborhood as they affect the school, an ethnocentric ideology from which both he and some of the parents suffer, and a conflict experienced by the principal concerning his accustomed role and the role being forced upon him by political and social pressures today. We shall now turn to a discussion of how each of these factors influenced the situation.

THE SOCIAL FORCES AT WORK
IN THE NEIGHBORHOOD

An examination of Mr. Fields' letter would indicate that he viewed the Slater area in stereotyped terms, conveying to his teachers a conception of the *de facto* segregated neighborhood as a homogeneous, deprived group. He failed to convey to them a picture that he may have known to exist—notice the frequent use of such modifying adjectives as *some* and *many*—for the total effect of his description was quite negative. Instead of this one-sided picture, he would have been more accurate had he been more conscious of, and more alert to, the many levels that do exist in urban areas today and specifically do exist in the given area.

There are several historical factors that can be pointed to as accounting for the heterogeneity of the Slater area. White immigrant groups have been aided in their assimilation into American life by the possibility of physical dispersion out of the residential ghetto. The first half of the century saw this happen at a rapid rate, aided by the availability of undeveloped land at the outskirts of cities. This physical dispersion has not been characteristic of the Negroes who have populated the northern cities in such large numbers since World War I and World War II.[1] The patterns of housing segregation are well known and will not be considered here. Only recently, and very slowly, has this pattern of segregation begun to break down.

Thus, in the city, the Negro neighborhood is likely to contain people of many economic and social classes living fairly close to one another. As new housing developed within the old Negro residential ghetto near Slater, the changes in residence did not occur along color lines but rather along class lines, and the neighborhood remains a *de facto* segregated one.

Skyview Terrace has become the home of working-class and lower-middle-class families selected on the basis of the middle-class view of propriety—working male as legal head of household and on the basis of modest economic success. Those who have chosen to live here are proud of their

[1] Karl E. Taeuber and Alma Taeuber, "The Negro as an Immigrant Group," *American Journal of Sociology, 69*, January (1964), 374-382.

positions and the outward signs of status gained by residence here as opposed to the old tenements in which they
used to live. We have seen how cleverly the rental appeals
were couched in terms to attract just such a group. Although
able to separate themselves physically from the slums, the
residents were still marginal in that many had to struggle
to maintain precarious grips on their new status. They bitterly resented any inference that they and their children
lacked ambition, ability, or morality.

This group prided itself on having been able to move
away from areas of dilapidated housing into the attractive
Skyview Terrace apartments. Recent examination of
working-class populations suggest that the family system is
very important to them.[2] The working-class families at
Slater do not choose to send their children out of the neighborhood to nonsegregated schools, preferring to keep them
close to home. They strongly support schooling for their
children, but they were very upset by what they viewed as
Mr. Fields' attack on the family, and they resent anything
that classifies them as "lower class." Intensely sensitive to
any implication that they represent a deprived—a word
they frequently fear is used to mean depraved—group,
these parents want no inferior education for their children,
which they anticipate when the children are categorized as
underprivileged. They do not wish their children to be
thought of in a condescending manner and are unimpressed
by principals who consider themselves dedicated for having
remained in the area, such dedication being viewed as pa-
ternalistic treatment and frowned upon. What they ask for is
the education they consider the children's due and resent any
implication that the youngsters are incapable of learning.

Poor school achievement is looked upon by the civil-rights
movement as an inadequacy on the school's part. Increasing
pressures are being brought to bear by the newly active

[2] Herbert J. Gans, *The Urban Villagers: Group and Class in the Life of Italian-Americans* (New York: The Free Press, 1962), pp. 244-245.

P.T.A.—which draws its militant members from the Negro residents of the new housing development—for the school to provide improved educational programs for the children. Sharing many of the goals and ideals of the larger American society concerning the desirability of social mobility, but confined to the residential ghetto because of pigmentation, restricted by lower economic status, and thus dependent upon public education, this group has adopted the view that superior education, or at least education equal to that of the white "middle-class" children, is the way through which the American mobility pattern will become open to them. To this group, Mr. Fields' description of the children as the offspring of poverty, with the concomitant deprivation assigned to it, represented an outright insult that warranted an apology.

In addition to the residents of Skyview, the area is beginning to contain numbers of middle-class Negro families who have achieved enough economic success to enable them to purchase apartments in the new cooperative housing being constructed. It was seen that there were indications that such families try to avoid sending their children to the public schools, choosing private or parochial instruction instead. Schooling is of great importance to such families, as noted in recent studies of the middle and upper-middle classes throughout the American population.[3] Why the parents choose nonpublic education is bound up again with the demand for higher standards for their children—the higher status symbols involved, plus the increased physical separation from the lower- and working-class populations. Should substantial numbers of children from this group enter the public school, school officials can anticipate accelerated parental activity regarding the school program and its results, just as has been true in the white middle- and upper-middle-class neighborhoods that this principal has avoided.

The area of dilapidated housing from which Mr. Fields

[3] *Ibid.,* pp. 246-249.

receives most of his "problems" did not actively take part in this protest, although indications of dissatisfaction with the school are evinced in the refusal to conform to the school's standards on the part of some children and the reluctance of some parents to be involved when they are summoned to the school to discuss complaints. It hardly seems necessary to explain why parents do this. When the school constantly confronts one with shame or failure, repeatedly implying that the failure is one of the individual or family rather than that of the school personnel or its program, such avoidance is to be expected. To infer from this that parents are "irresponsible" or do not care about their children is fallacious. Unless opportunities are provided for such children and parents to view the school as providing meaningful, successful experiences and feelings of personal dignity or worth, the school and its leaders are likely to be viewed as outright enemies. Later in this study we shall explore some of the factors that help to account for this serious gulf between the schools and some "lower-class" people, making for mutual frustration concerning the educational experience.

Although an understanding of class differences in the neighborhood sheds some light on the reactions of people to the school, this particular event cannot be viewed without reference to the extreme awareness concerning racial attitudes that is evident here. Particularly offensive to the complaining parents was the negative picture of the children presented by Mr. Fields. Already sensitive to this kind of description, as can be noticed in the petition and in the way in which the parents approached and attacked the principal, they answered with almost a denial that any of the conditions he described did actually exist in the area, a view that is unrealistic but common. Why then were they so offended?

Interestingly enough, the complaining parents agreed that the new teachers would be unfamiliar with Negroes. However, and this is significant, they believed that what the new teachers would know about Negroes would in good measure have been just the kind of negative picture Mr. Fields was presenting. Thus, in the press, in the literature on the disadvantaged, and through hearsay, the teachers would have been exposed almost daily to the same sensational view of the destitute group that the principal was describing, for the Negro population more often than not is identified with its "problem" element. Those who escape the problems of the "lower class" feel them as a close threat.[4] People of dark skin color and of low status not only are often viewed in American society as being economically deprived, despite the large numbers who are not, but such economic deprivation is frequently automatically but incorrectly associated with emotional deprivation and immorality.

The portion of the Negro community, and the view of Negro life, with which the new teachers would probably be unfamiliar was precisely that section that took offense at Mr. Fields's letter. To these parents, that letter was seen as reinforcing the ignorance and prejudice concerning themselves held by white people. And an important implication of this, as far as the parents were concerned, was that this kind of negativism would continually serve to diminish the teachers' aspirations for pupils' achievement. Indeed, his welcoming remarks did imply that those teachers who had stayed in his school had lost some of their spirit.[5] His later remarks were not calculated to preserve the spirit of the newcomers. As one parent put it, "If I were a young, white, middle-class girl, and was handed that letter, I wouldn't even take the job."

In brief, then, the principal's clash with the parents arose

[4] Nathan Glazer and Daniel Patrick Moynihan, *Beyond the Melting Pot* (Cambridge, Mass.: The M.I.T. Press, 1963), p. 51.
[5] See Howard S. Becker, "The Career of the Chicago Public School Teacher," *American Journal of Sociology,* 17 (1952), 470-476, for an interesting description of the adjustments made by teachers who stay in slum-area schools.

partly out of his incomplete understanding of the goals and
needs of the people in the neighborhood. Because in the
contemporary American scene incidents concerning race
relations and education cannot be seen apart from the
wider economic, political, and social changes taking place,
Mr. Fields found himself in the newspapers and a subject
for discussion among civil-rights groups. However, this
alone does not explain the position in which he found himself, nor does it adequately explain his message to the teachers, for even had the neighborhood been as "deprived" as he
made it appear, he would have been likely to run into conflict. For an understanding of this we must turn to a
discussion of the value system that he brought to the situation, a value system widely held by other personnel working with similar school populations.

VALUES

Anthropologists have long been cognizant of the phenomenon of ethnocentrism: the tendency to be so rooted in
one's own cultural experience that one's own way of life is
preferred to all others. Although one does not necessarily
move from this preference toward a disdainful view of other
ways of life, it is relatively easy to do so. Even more, it can
lead to a denial of any value in the ways of others.

There is nothing new about this tendency to evaluate people differently from ourselves. When Caesar visited Britain
he considered the inhabitants "barbarian." Later, when the
British and other western Europeans, representing the most
advanced industrial nations, set out to construct a world
empire, they viewed the people they met as a *tabula rasa*
—devoid of any culture and awaiting the gift of Western
civilization. The White Man's Burden and the French Civ-
ilizing Mission were expressions of this point of view, which
ignored the histories and cultures of peoples throughout
the world.

In a recent study of schools in an American Indian community, Murray and Rosalie Wax describe the ways in which this ethnocentric viewpoint has affected education. They have defined the phenomenon as the "Vacuum Ideology."

> By "Vacuum Ideology" we mean the disposition of administrators and school officials to support policies and programs (such as the establishment of nursery schools) with the assertion that the Indian home and the mind of the Indian child are meager, empty or lacking in pattern.[6]

Although at Slater we are dealing with variation within the larger American culture, rather than with a cross-cultural situation, we can observe how this feeling of superiority and moral virtue assigned to one's own position in society can lead to an adoption of the *tabula rasa* or "Vacuum Ideology" view toward different ethnic or class groups.

Mr. Fields has used traits, pulled out of context, to describe the "deprived" segment of Slater's population, preparing his teachers to expect their charges to be "not ready for school when they enter" because they are coming from ". . . a poor environment, socially, culturally, economically, physically . . ."

This view assumes that poverty and social, cultural, emotional, and academic deprivation are synonymous. We do not here mean to glorify poverty—only those outside it can view the state as romantic, although it is more often viewed as repulsive. It is necessary to point out, however, that not everyone on welfare is there because of apathy or lack of encouragement to achieve. Families on welfare are there because of prolonged illness, death of parents, old age, seasonal unemployment, and, more important, lack of job skills in our age of accelerated automation, for which large

---

[6] Murray L. Wax, Rosalie H. Wax, *et al.,* "Formal Education in an American Indian Community," Supplement to *Social Problems,* Vol. 2, No. 4 (Spring 1964).

numbers of the American people have simply not been prepared. Relatively recent migration from rural areas plus a long history of discrimination in employment and job training have made Negroes particularly vulnerable to the ravages of technological unemployment.

Furthermore, welfare reflects an income status. One must remember that welfare or qualification for free lunch is not synonymous with lack of organized family life, although a family may not consist of the ideal middle-class version of father, mother, and children. Nor does welfare or different family form necessarily mean an absence of healthy interpersonal relations or even the absence of satisfying meals at home. The middle class too has its share of fatherless households, high divorce rate, alcoholism, and drug addiction, as well as questionable eating habits, for these are not confined to the lower classes.[7] It is essential to remember that, to the individual child, the severe emotional deprivation that interferes with learning is not a class matter. Of course, those children who suffer both economic and emotional deprivation face formidable problems. We must be cautious, however, and not automatically connect economic deprivation with emotional and cultural deprivation. To do so would be to impose an ethnocentric view of the lower class that can succeed only in further alienating the school from the people so dependent upon it for training in this era of our history.

Children who are different, in that their manners, speech, and beliefs vary from those of the people who run the schools, are not without experience and emotions and verbal abilities that, if recognized and respected and not re-

[7] This view of the tendency to judge the lower class against an ideal version of the middle class concurs with a discussion of the problem presented by Eleanor Leacock and Constance Sutton, "Authoritarianism and Class Culture" presented at the fifty-ninth annual meeting of the American Anthropological Society, Minneapolis, 1960.

jected as shameful or wrong, can be utilized for an improved school experience.

In their study, the Waxes further found that, occasionally, educational administrators profess to be interested in the backgrounds of their pupils, but when action is undertaken, the needs of the bureaucracy tend to be redefined as efforts at instilling into the children convenient habits or attitudes—attending regularly and respecting property and school personnel—implying that if only the children would obey the rules they would be educated.[8] Mr. Fields had done the same thing. He had become interested in studies of lower-class populations, but he used the social-science concepts and descriptions, not only out of context and inappropriately, but also as a means of rationalizing the *status quo* approach to the children, an approach that has already failed. He has used the social-science data in support of his middle-class view of the "lower class," a thing few of the social scientists would do or want done with their findings.

The comments that fill the letter are drawn from professional literature dealing with the problems of children in low socioeconomic areas, and within their proper context are generally accepted to be effective working descriptions. In the history of education they appear to represent an advance over earlier concepts that held that children did not achieve because of low capability.

The group intelligence-quotient score, for example, until relatively recently was viewed by educators as an indication of innate capability. As our mass education system has come to encompass larger and larger numbers of young people, educators have been forced to examine the reasons for the vast numbers of unsuccessful scholars. Also, no educator has been happy with the numbers of reluctant scholars, unwilling and often unwanted, who by their apathy or

---

[8] Wax and Wax, *op. cit.*, pp. 62-64.

hostility have interfered with the traditional routines of teaching, creating situations tantamount to cold wars in innumerable classrooms throughout the land. Why has such social distance between many of our educators and their pupils developed? Why has the school experience proved a frustration for teacher and pupil? Why are so many pupils unsuccessful? Traditional intelligence tests could not provide the answer.

In an effort to explore these questions more fully, professional studies in recent years have sought to understand better the school population we now have in our urban centers. There is frequent reference to economic, sociological, anthropological, or psychological traits to explain the nature of academically unsuccessful children. Mr. Fields' letter was sprinkled with this terminology—"disadvantaged," "welfare," "lacking a male image," "high hearing level," "characteristics of poverty," "ethnic differences."[9] This language represents a serious effort on the part of social scientists and educators to understand more fully the problems faced by certain segments of the population in relation to the school experience and requires careful study by those involved with education as a basis for positive programs. However, certain dangers exist that must be avoided.

We have already discussed one danger, the use of this knowledge in support of the middle-class view of the lower class and in support of traditional programs that have not been noted for their success. Another danger that exists is that of applying the traits to populations they do not fit. Populations who do not wish to be so described may also react negatively. We have seen how Mr. Fields did this at Slater and have seen how quickly the parents rose in indignation. The third danger, and perhaps most serious, is that ascribing these traits to populations might be used in

[9] Among the investigators whose work influenced the content of Mr. Fields' letter are Martin Deutsch, Oscar Lewis, Frank Reissman, and Harry Passow.

itself to justify or to excuse inadequate educational programs that have failed to raise pupil achievement levels. This is one of the things so frightening to people who fall within or close to the categories described.

The terminology, so useful and illuminating to the professional social scientist, when used as it was in the Slater letter emphasizes all the obstacles and thus appears to the parents to anticipate, and thereby practically to ensure, failure. To dismiss this reaction as hypersensitive and unreasonable is to fail to recognize that the reactions of the parents are an indication of a desperate urgency that their children be caught up in the mainstream of the American mobility pattern, the key to which is seen to be educational achievement. It is an indication that the parents do not believe that their children will be receiving the kind of schooling necessary for this from negatively oriented teachers.

There is another way in which Mr. Fields' views affected his relations with the parents. We have seen that the letter to his teachers was regarded as evidence of his attitude toward the neighborhood, the parents, and the children, resulting in the call for his dismissal by some parents. How true is this charge? Can Mr. Fields be said to have been bigoted? Certainly he would vigorously deny this. Having served in the Slater area fourteen years, fully intending to remain here until his retirement, he viewed himself as a faithful public servant, doing all he could to run a good school. He vigorously contested any implications that his school was denying educational advantages to the children who attended. To those who argued that a *de facto* segregated school was necessarily inferior, Mr. Fields would retort that it was an insult to minority-group children to feel that they could not achieve except by rubbing shoulders with the children of nonsegregated areas. He strongly felt that the lack of achievement in school was not a function of school inadequacy, but rather the function of problems the school could not control. Thus, in his letter he wrote ". . . for there are certain responsibilities that the community must assume and not purge itself of a sense of guilt by criticizing the schools."

The charge of bigotry is strong, and it does not fruitfully describe the situation. Like everyone else, Mr. Fields has a set of values that he has brought with him, which affect the way in which he thinks, observes, and works. One of the values he holds is typically "middle class" American. It amounts to the belief that effort is good in itself and that with effort one is rewarded with success. This thinking is based on the view that the universe is mechanistic and man is its master. Thus man can improve himself by controlling the universe about him.[10] In regard to minority-group failure in achievement, Mr. Fields would hold that this failure is a function of lack of effort and lack of taking advantage of available opportunity, and thus the low achievement of the children in his school is viewed as a function of personal responsibility rather than of a lack of school effort. Throughout American life and particularly among the middle class runs this theme that doing something about a condition or problem will almost invariably bring success in solving it and that obstacles exist to be overcome.

These views also permeate the lives of individuals. Thus, those who do not succeed have not made adequate "effort" and are relegated to a position of inferiority or failure. Serious effort to achieve success is viewed not only as a personal goal but also as a moral imperative. "It indicates a culture in which effort is rewarded, competition enforced, merit and personal achievement recognized."[11] As a moral

[10] Cora DuBois, "The Dominant Value Profile of American Culture," *American Anthropologist*, 57 (1955), 1232-1239.
[11] Conrad Arensberg and Arthur Niehoff, *Introducing Social Change* (Chicago: Aldine Publishing Co., 1964), p. 166.

code this is immensely severe. The problems such a code raises are enormous, for those in positions of achievement are successes, whereas those in low positions are viewed as failures—failures who are viewed as being such as a consequence of their own personal inadequacy or lack of drive to achieve.

Mr. Fields is a strong believer in these values. His own career pattern attests to his firm belief that with hard work and effort one can achieve a high position and success. Thus, although the son of poor immigrants, he worked his way through school, earned degrees, and attained the position of principal that, to his generation, during the Depression, represented a very high status and still does to a degree.

Not only has he "made it" up the ladder of success, but he also has made frequent reference to ethnic groups that have succeeded in America; he has seen a whole generation of immigrants' children rise above the economic and social status from which they started. He believes that Negro and Puerto Rican groups can achieve the same successes as other Americans if only they would make the effort involved. Thus he views their failure as a function of their selves. This point of view is widely held among Americans.

Yet such a point of view ignores the position of the Negro in American life. The barriers that have led to a denial of opportunity cannot be equated with the obstacles confronting white immigrants. The color line has been basic to American social structure, the Negro occupying a caste-like position. It is important to remember that large sections of the Slater area are also imbued with the value system described as middle-class American and are desperately searching to destroy the caste-like restrictions that they have faced throughout their history in America. Effort toward achievement is increasingly accepted as the meaningful value to be

pursued in life, and here, as throughout the Negro community in America, education is highly valued.[12] Recent
studies of the American class structure have pointed to variations in specific goals pursued and styles of life,[13] but
we must remember that in all groups the influence of the
larger American value system operates. In addition, large
sections of Negro America as well as white have become
increasingly aware of the employment problems evolving
from automation, the economic value of education is recognized, and large amounts of propaganda against dropping
out of school are being disseminated. Increasing opportunities do exist for crossing the old caste barriers in employment and schooling. More and more parents recognize
that, even if the caste walls were to come tumbling down,
their children would still need the skills to climb over the
rubble. The past decade has seen the demands for full
participation in American life extended, from the civil-
rights movement to the demands for improved education
in the North. Responses of endurance, pessimism, acceptance, pliancy, and evasion are viewed with contempt by
those seeking full equality of opportunity.

We have seen that, although the parents of the Slater children chose to keep their children near home, rather than
send them to schools out of the neighborhood, they remained very watchful over all events in the school, no longer
the passive, seemingly apathetic parent body Mr. Fields en-
countered when he first came to the neighborhood fourteen
years ago.

It must be noted that the parental pressures he now

[12] See Norval D. Glenn, "Negro Prestige Criteria: A Case Study in the
Phases of Prestige," *American Journal of Sociology*, 68 (1963), 645-647,
for a discussion of the prestige accorded educational achievement in American Negro Life. Also see Max Weiner and Walter Murray, "Another Look
at the Culturally Deprived and Their Levels of Aspiration," *Journal of
Educational Sociology*, March 1963, pp. 319-321.

[13] Gans, op. cit., pp. 229-262.

faced cannot be dismissed as the work of a small minority. First of all, the large attendance during Open School Week attests to widespread parent interest. However, an even more important point must be made. Great social movements, even revolutions, are not necessarily the work of a majority. A numerical minority, with an articulate leadership and an ideology, can effect great changes. It would be a mistake to interpret the call for the dismissal of the principal as an unimportant thing. It was symptomatic of feeling in the neighborhood, and, in addition, indicated that the person running the local elementary school was not attuned to the needs of the residents.

It was also a reflection of growing questions concerning whether or not the school was performing as competent an educational job as this principal believed, for a merely efficient school could no longer meet the needs of the day. Times had changed; the parents had developed new aspirations and organizational efforts to that end. The function of Slater was being viewed differently, but Mr. Fields had not himself been fully aware of the rapid changes that were occurring, changes that were forcing new perspectives and new roles upon him.

ROLE OF THE PRINCIPAL

Social scientists recognize that all individuals in society occupy many positions, each of these being called a "status." The anthropologist Ralph Linton defined status as a position in the social system. Role was defined as the patterned behavior that the particular culture associates with the status.[14] Thus, for example, in our culture the status of physician carries with it the role of treatment of the sick.

Robert K. Merton, the sociologist, has further developed

[14] Ralph Linton, *The Study of Man* (New York: Appleton-Century-Crofts, 1936), pp. 113-131.

the concept of status and role. He points out that each status position in reality has associated with it not one but many roles. He calls this the "role-set," defining it as that "complement of role relationships in which persons are involved by virtue of occupying a particular status."[15] The role-set of the physician might include interaction with patients, doctor colleagues, nurses, hospital attendants, hospital administrative staff, and patients' families, among others.

Mr. Fields is a principal. This is the status in which we have met him. Although he fills many other status positions in society—husband and father, for example—it is as principal that he functions in the Slater area. The role-set of an elementary-school principal involves a great number of relationships. Relationships with parents, children, teachers, community groups, the assistant superintendent, custodial staff, other principals, and other members of the Board of Education are among these.

Principals are generally aware that they must deal with varying groups of people. They are also generally aware of how they are expected to behave by those in positions of greater power than themselves within the role-set. For example, principals anticipate and respond to Board of Education directives and generally keep their supervisors informed concerning events. However, there is a tendency to view the entire role-set as hierarchically arranged. Thus principals do not always expect their behavior to be viewed critically by others in the role-set who are viewed as having less power than themselves. We have seen that in his letter Mr. Fields ordered the teachers to direct the children, and he described plans to direct the parents. He reacted with indignation when the parents displayed a different perception of how he should have behaved toward them. The sud-

---

[15] Robert K. Merton, "The Role Set: Problems in Sociological Theory," *British Journal of Sociology*, 8 (June 1957), 110. This entire article is recommended for further discussion.

den display of power on the part of the parents, a group he viewed as low on the hierarchical scale, came as a rude shock to him.

As we examine the role-set concept, it becomes evident that persons or groups viewing the principal may have differing and even conflicting expectations of the conduct appropriate for him. At Slater the principal viewed a letter to his teachers as providing proper guidance. The parents, on the other hand, viewed the letter quite differently. The reason for the differing views is to be found in the social position held by the Negro parents, a social position different from that held by the principal. Merton has described this source of conflict for role-set members.

> The basic source of this potential for conflict, I suggest . . . is that the members of a role-set are, to some degree, apt to hold social positions differing from that of the occupant of the status in question. To the extent that they are diversely located in the social structure, they are apt to have interests and sentiments, values and moral expectations differing from those of the status-occupant himself.[16]

Another point of conflict between Mr. Fields and the parents must be adduced. The neighborhood of Slater was where the parents lived and had their private lives. The principal did not live there. Neither did most of the teachers. To the principal and the teachers, the Slater area was where they worked. They did not have their private lives there but rather were known in the neighborhood by their work statuses.

Solon Kimball and James E. McClellan, in their book *Education and the New America*,[17] have described the school as functioning to move the child from the private life of the

16 *Ibid.,* p. 112.

17 Solon Kimball and James E. McClellan, *Education and the New America* (New York: Random House, 1962).

family to the world of school and teacher, and eventually into the public world of work. Mr. Fields received the children into the school and proceeded, in the parents' view, to attack the private world of the family. Calling for his ouster as principal, the parents rallied against him and attacked him in the public world of work, where he derived his prestige.

Not only do different members of the role-set view a principal with differing expectations, but views of the members may sometimes be in conflict with one another. Indeed this is increasingly the case in urban areas, where militant community groups have come into conflict with boards of education concerning school integration problems. Sometimes this results in attacks upon school principals, despite what the latter consider to be effective functioning on their part. Many an innocent school head may find himself a target in the battle between parents and boards of education or even between conflicting groups of parents.

It would appear that, where there is a great deal of conflict, the principal's position is an untenable one. Fortunately this need not be the case, providing he does not hold rigidly to a conception of his role inappropriate for a period of social change.

Several mechanisms exist to permit the principal to resolve the conflicts he is facing. One of these was noted by Mr. Fields himself when he said he should not have given a letter meant for his teachers to the parents. Sociologists call this "the concept of privileged information and confidential communication."[18] However, although one might agree that the parents need not know everything said to the teachers, observability of the principal's behavior is desirable. It serves as a check and can highlight areas of disagreement that require resolution, as at Slater.

[18] Merton, op. cit., p. 115.

A more constructive mechanism available to the principal is concerned and interested observation of the demands of members of the role-set. Thus he can make known to the Board of Education the desires of the parents, plus the needs of the children and the teachers, and can leave it to the board to solve the problems. At the very least, this approach lays the foundation for a more objective appraisal by the principal of the social forces affecting the school and himself as its head.

An added support for the principal comes from others in the same status. Membership in a professional organization of principals becomes important. Thus, although problems remain unsolved, colleagues with similar woes give one another moral support. Together their strength as a pressure group is increased. Together they are in a better position to explore the causes of and solutions to problems.

A negative solution available is for the principal to leave his position. Mr. Fields did not choose to do this. Some principals have, however, by bidding a bitter farewell to a career or by seeking a different assignment.

The events at Slater illustrate some of the intense stresses felt by the principals of urban schools in our time. We have already seen the shock with which Mr. Fields viewed the parents' reaction. We have also seen his surprise at finding that his assistant superintendent and the representatives from the Board of Education did not fully support him in opposition to the parents but rather played the part of conciliators.

For fourteen years Mr. Fields functioned as a principal without serious difficulty. Then he found that social pressures were forcing him to examine his role, for serious disequilibrium had set in.

Mr. Fields viewed his position as principal as requiring that he be an efficient manager of a school plant and its personnel. He had to fulfill the requirements that the bureaucratic school system imposed on him. Thus he stressed such factors as attendance, orderliness, and care of property and prided himself on a smoothly running school. The emphasis placed by school administrators on these matters is not atypical, and the reasons for its being found in American schools have been amply documented.

Raymond S. Callahan, in his book *Education and the Cult of Efficiency*, has traced the influence of admirers of businessmen and industrialists who created an emphasis upon the technical, financial, and mechanical aspects of education in the leading graduate schools of the country. With some exceptions, the social and philosophical sides of education have been neglected in the training of school administrators. Our public schools bear the legacy of concepts of organization and plant utilization, modeled after factories rather than after centers of learning.[19]

Mr. Fields also saw himself as the paternal head of the school. We noticed how he felt responsible for his teachers and their orientation, how he was a sympathetic, friendly figure, yet stern in his instructions to them.

In addition, Mr. Fields, a middle-class intellectual himself, regarded himself as holding a sacred trust—that of passing the cultural heritage of society on to another generation fairly intact. Thus, he viewed with a deep sense of disturbance the inability of some of his school population to succeed academically, although he did not view their failure as a function of inadequacy in the educational program he provided.

The parents, on the other hand, viewed the principal as holding the key to the gates that they felt locked their children out of the mainstream of American life. To the parents, Mr. Fields personified the educational system that more and more people today are imbuing with the magic

---

[19] Raymond S. Callahan, *Education and the Cult of Efficiency* (Chicago: University of Chicago Press, 1962), pp. 179-220.

power to erase poverty, delinquency, immorality, mental illness, and assorted other ills facing society. This almost pathetic faith in the healing powers of education pervades the nation. Administrators believe that if only children will attend school and obey the rules they will be educated, and people are increasingly expecting of the schools an assured ride on the escalator toward fullfillment of the American dream of well-being and happiness for all.

This faith in education has caused the protesting parents' to decry the stereotyped notion of Negro life, for, as seen, they hold upward-mobility ambitions and do not want to be denied equal training. At the same time, it is unrealistic to deny that the school is finding itself failing, for its traditional program and approach have not been successful with many of the pupils, particularly those from the lower social class.

To charge the school with the solution of all our ills is of course highly unrealistic, for schools have no control over the economic forces that have created the mass of unskilled and marginal workers in our cities, resulting from the automation of farm and factory, who fill the ranks of the unemployed. Yet we must begin somewhere, and the schools remain the agency of society that moves the children from family to readiness for participation in public life and the world of work. The school in contemporary America is being charged with containing vast numbers of those who in a previous era would have been allowed to leave to perform unskilled labor in the city and on the farm. A school system that was adequate in a previous era will not do today, for, with the acceleration of industrial change, such jobs no longer exist in sufficient number. Unless the school can succeed in its task of preparing members of the lower social classes, large numbers of Negroes and others will be left further and further behind as more and more training is required for employment and upward mobility in our century.

The events at Slater suggest that educational programs and the people directing them must maintain standards, programs, and facilities at a high level for children, regardless of social status. There is evidence that low-income children have not, over the years, been receiving equal facilities,[20] and those facilities being provided now hardly begin to make up for the years of educational deprivation provided by the school system itself. The evidence simply does not justify relieving the schools of their responsibility in the matter. Any educational program that does not provide as full a share of facilities and as high an aspirational level for Negroes as for any other children will be viewed with increasingly intense hostility. This explains in part the demands for school integration in the North as well as in the South, for many Negro leaders feel that only when white children are also involved will the schools provide truly equal education.

What of the "lower class" from which Mr. Fields and other principals feel they get so many of their "problems" and serious academic failures? Again, there must be caution against the automatic assignment of social and academic deprivation and of depravity or immorality to the state of poverty. The middle-class tendency to judge this class according to an ethnocentric view of the ideal conditions of the middle class as against the real conditions in the lower class leads to a distorted perspective and increased social distance between lower-class children and parents and school personnel. We would suggest that contemporary urban life, with its vast communications system making for increasingly shared extrafamilial experience, has brought the middle-, working-, and lower-class child closer together. The number of lower-class children who do not present

[20] Patricia A. Sexton, *Education and Income* (New York: Viking Press, 1961).

"problems" to the school and who do achieve attest to this. Although we as yet lack adequate empirical data, several studies are underway that seek to identify the factors that enable such children to achieve within our school system.[21]

For those children who appear so different to educators that traditional approaches and techniques have failed, bold new programs must be designed to bridge the barriers that have alienated the children and the schools from each other. The very first step in this direction is a genuine respect for the dignity of each child and each parent, regardless of how different they are from school personnel. Any view that persists in assigning shame to lower-class status is designed to alienate further those who either find they cannot pull themselves out of this class because of forces beyond their control or who choose to retain their class identifications. This alienation results in the inability of the individual to respect himself and his potential or in overt hostility to the school.

Administrators and teachers assigned to deal with minority-group populations have to re-evaluate their roles in order to function more appropriately in schools in the midst of social change. Many of the symbols and methods that have been regarded as essential to their occupations may have to be abandoned. Indeed, it may not be possible for many to abandon their old style and impossible to develop empathy and acceptance for people viewed as different from themselves. But a positive approach to teaching the previously unsuccessful is essential. This requires a revamped training program that not only acquaints the profession with the problems and cultural patterns of the school population, as they are unearthed by social-science research

[21] Two such studies are being conducted by Bernard Mackler at the Institute of Urban Studies, Teachers College, and Helen Davidson and Judith Greenberg at City College of the City University, New York.

as a basis for positive programs, but also provides training in the uses of such data, as well as training in the establishment of genuine rapport—rapport in which people are neither blamed nor patronized because of conditions they cannot control.

BIBLIOGRAPHY

Arensberg, Conrad, and Arthur Niehoff. *Introducing Social Change: A Manual for Americans Overseas.* Chicago: Aldine Publishing Co., 1964.

Becker, Howard S. "The Career of the Chicago Public School Teacher," *American Journal of Sociology,* 57 (1952), 470–477.

Callahan, Raymond S. *Education and the Cult of Efficiency.* Chicago: University of Chicago Press, 1962.

Clark, Kenneth B. "Segregated Schools in New York City," *Journal of Educational Sociology* (February 1963), pp. 245–250.

Deutsch, Martin P. *Minority Group and Class Status as Related to Social and Personality Factors in Scholastic Achievement.* Ithaca, N.Y.: Society for Applied Anthropology, Monograph No. 2, 1960.

DuBois, Cora. "The Dominant Value Profile of American Culture," *American Anthropologist,* 57 (1955), 1232–1239.

Duhl, Leonard J. *The Urban Condition.* New York: Basic Books, 1963.

Frazier, E. Franklin. *Black Bourgeoisie: Rise of a New*

Middle Class in the United States. New York: The Free Press, 1957.

————*The Negro in the United States.* New York: The Macmillan Company, 1949.

Gans, Herbert J. *The Urban Villagers: Group and Class in the Life of Italian-Americans.* New York: The Free Press, 1962.

Glazer, Nathan, and Daniel Patrick Moynihan. *Beyond the the Melting Pot.* Cambridge, Mass.: Harvard University Press, 1963.

Glenn, Norval D. "Negro Prestige Criteria: A Case Study in the Phases of Prestige," *The American Journal of Sociology,* 68 (1963), 645–657.

Goode, William J. "A Theory of Role Strain," *American Sociological Review,* 25 (1960), 483–496.

Handlin, Oscar. "Is Integration the Answer?" *Atlantic Monthly,* 213 (March 1964), 49–54.

Harrington, Michael. *The Other America.* New York: The Macmillan Company, 1963.

Hoffer, Eric. "The Negro Is Prejudiced Against Himself," *New York Times Magazine,* November 29, 1964.

Kimball, Solon, and James E. McClellan. *Education and the New America.* New York: Random House, 1962.

Leacock, Eleanor, and Constance Sutton. "Authoritarianism and Class Culture," speech presented at the fifty-ninth annual meeting of the American Anthropological Association, Minneapolis, 1960.

Linton, Ralph. *The Study of Man.* New York: Appleton-Century-Crofts, 1936.

Lystad, Mary H. "Family Patterns, Achievements, and Aspirations of Urban Negroes," *Sociology and Social Research,* 45 (1961), 281–288.

Merton, Robert K. "The Role Set: Problems in Sociological Theory," *British Journal of Sociology,* 8 (June 1957), 106–120.

Passow, A. Harry. *Education in Depressed Areas.* New York: Bureau of Publications, Teachers College, Columbia University, 1963.

Riessman, Frank. *The Culturally Deprived Child.* New York: Harper & Row, 1962.

Sexton, Patricia A. *Education and Income.* New York: Viking Press, 1961.

Taeuber, Karl E., and Alma F. Taeuber. "The Negro as an Immigrant Group," *American Journal of Sociology,* 69 No. 4 (January 1964), 374–382.

Wax, Murray L., Rosalie H. Wax, *et al.* "Formal Education in an American Indian Community," Supplement to *Social Problems,* 2, No. 4 (Spring 1964).

Weiner, Max, and Walter Murray. "Another Look at the Culturally Deprived and Their Levels of Aspiration," *Journal of Educational Sociology* (March 1963), pp. 319–321.

Young, Whitney. "Education and Artificiality," *Amsterdam News,* September 19, 1964.

PART TWO

SCHOOL BOYCOTT: EDUCATION IN THE STREETS

Political democracy, as it exists and practically works in America, with all its threatening evils, supplies a training-school for making first-class men. It is life's gymnasium, not of good only, but of all. We try often, though we fall back often. A brave delight, fit for freedom's athletes, fills these arenas, and fully satisfies, out of the action in them, irrespective of success. Whatever we do not attain, we at any rate attain the experiences of the fight, the hardening of the strong campaign, and throb with currents of attempt at least.

WALT WHITMAN, *Democratic Vistas*

INTRODUCTION

"SCHOOL BOYCOTT," Part Two, is an examination of one boycott directed against *de facto* school segregation in the North. "Operation Shutdown," which became popularly known as the "600" School Boycott, took place in the early part of 1965, in New York City.

In its demands for improved schooling for Negroes, who constitute a major proportion of those who feel blocked from full equality, the civil-rights movement has collided full force with educators who are often at a loss to understand why they are so bitterly attacked. Also, to many educators it appears strange if not reprehensible that civil-rights leaders would ask children not to attend school.

But, to many in the civil-rights movement, the schools as they are do not seem appropriately organized or oriented to help achieve full equality, especially for Negroes. More important, perhaps, is the fact that many youngsters in the inner-city residential ghettos feel this way.

In our study we sought to examine in some detail Operation Shutdown, one example of social protest directed against a northern school system. Because we believe that this event cannot be understood outside its historical and social context, the study includes an examination of the Negro civil-rights movement and its struggle for what its leaders and participants believe to be the kind of educational system necessary to ensure full equality for Negroes in America. Interestingly enough, it has been more difficult to design a new educational program than it has been to document the failure of the old. There is no simple solution to the complex problems involved in making American schools function to permit Negroes of all classes and the urban poor, white as well as Negro, access to equal participation in the larger society. That our schools have been unable to reach many who face a bleak future in a cybernated America is apparent from the dropouts, truants, and behavior-problem children who characterize innumerable classrooms throughout the land. More significant perhaps, low achievement levels for youngsters living in the inner cities pose the dilemma of lack of preparation at the very time that the legal barriers to separation from the mainstream of American life have been removed by the civil-rights legislation of recent years.

The growth of school boycott activities in the nation seems to indicate that some school children see themselves victimized by the education system as it is now functioning and have begun to engage in protest activities directed at schools. In order to understand this more fully, in addition to the broader significance of school boycotts, we have sought to examine in some depth the reasons for participation in a school boycott and the effects of such participation on various youngsters involved. To do this, we gathered observations on events in the freedom schools, and we conducted depth interviews with teen-agers who had actively participated in the boycott. We explored several questions.

Among these were the following: How did you happen to join? What was the purpose of the boycott? Describe what happened. How did your family feel about your participating? How do you feel about segregated schools? Integrated schools? How do your friends feel about it? We also questioned the youths concerning their favorite teachers or those they disliked. We explored their knowledge and opinions concerning the civil-rights movement in the South. They told us about their ambitions. We asked them, too, what they felt they had learned from the boycott.

These youths talked about their experiences with great feeling and thoughtfulness. Many of the young people's comments are included in this study. Our informants, who were representative of teen-age participants in the boycott, ranged in age from fourteen to eighteen. They included high-school dropouts, a high-school senior who had been accepted by a well-known university and been awarded a scholarship, two junior-high-school girls, boys who had attended "600" schools, and boys who, although not dropouts from school, were still truant.

They were all youngsters who would ordinarily be classified in socioeconomic terms as "disadvantaged." In some cases there was no father at home; in others unemployment was present; in only one case was academic achievement high by the school's definition. Several youths had histories of delinquent-gang membership. All the informants were Negro and lived in a section of the city that was all Negro. All had attended *de facto* segregated elementary schools and junior high schools. Some, however, also attended high schools with integrated populations. Several had previous association with organized civil-rights groups. For others, the shutdown involved was their first civil-rights experience.

As their comments are read, it becomes clear that all shared a common dissatisfaction with current or past school experiences, as well as possessing an acute awareness of the subordinate position of the Negro in American life. These perceptions did not arise as a result of the boycott but preceded it, and the shutdown provided opportunity to express dissatisfaction with existing conditions. Thus the boycott provided a means of actively expressing social protest.

This study is not based on a statistical sampling of children involved in the boycott. Instead, using anthropological methodology, depth interviews were conducted with eleven youngsters who were intimately connected with Operation Shutdown and stayed with it until it ended. Admittedly, they were all active partisans of the boycott and had taken very active roles in it. The youngsters were contacted through adult boycott leaders. We explained to the informants that we were genuinely interested in hearing their side of the boycott story in order to increase understanding of what had happened. The interviews were held outside the formal school environment. In order to avoid introducing the element of race difference, the author, who is white, was assisted by a Negro social scientist, who did the actual interviews.

We are very much aware of the limitations of the research concerning these children. We regret not having complete life histories. It was not possible to check back carefully through school records and school personnel acquainted with the youngsters interviewed. We were, nevertheless, able to do such checking for some, and we found in all cases that our informants had been remarkably candid concerning their school records. We believe that the chief value of the presentation of the interview data lies in indicating the huge reservoir of ideas, perceptions, and emotions that youngsters have concerning school and about which we know too little.

The young people's views of the schools and teachers give

us some insights concerning their perceptions of the school environment. If the schools are to function successfully to help bridge the gap between lower status and full equality in American life, it is necessary to understand the impediments to that goal as viewed by the children themselves.

In addition to the depth interviews with children, we sought to explore the experiences that larger numbers had had in the various freedom schools set up to house boycotting pupils. In order to gain a picture of events there, various persons were interviewed, among them directors, teachers, student volunteer leaders, landlords, and attendance personnel responsible for returning the children to public school. Press accounts, including those from the *Amsterdam News, New York Times, World Telegram and Sun, Daily News, and National Guardian* were examined. Freedom-school literature was also read.

Chapter 4, "Uniting for Conflict," which includes material on freedom schools, was not intended to be an exhaustive study of these schools. Furthermore, there was no attempt to do a comparative study within the city or with schools established during boycotts elsewhere. The freedom schools that functioned during Operation Shutdown provided the organizational context, the milieu in which our informants moved, and for that reason it became necessary to provide a description of them.[1]

The author personally observed picket lines at schools and at the Board of Education. In addition, civil-rights leaders and public-school personnel were interviewed. Pertinent literature and official publications were also consulted.

School boycotts directed against the *de facto* segregated school systems of the North are an increasing problem for

---

[1] There is a growing body of information concerning freedom schools and their functioning in this country. This is an area in which research is very much needed.

American education today. This study is one effort aimed at understanding the conflicts. Hopefully, school personnel, by studying those who feel strongly enough to walk out of school by dropping out entirely or boycotting temporarily, can learn much about themselves and the children whom they would teach in this era of social change.

The Background

1. SCHOOL CONFLICT IN THE CITY

I T IS A PARODOX of our time that public schools designed to provide equal opportunity for all according to their ability have found themselves the objects of civil-rights pickets who regard these same schools as operating to deny equality of educational opportunity. Protests have not been limited to the *de jure* segregated schools of the South. Conflicts between the civil rights movement and *de facto* segregated northern school systems are increasingly frequent. New York, Cleveland, Chicago, and Milwaukee, among other cities boasting large and advanced school systems, have found themselves confronted with boycotts protesting *de facto* segregation and the inferior education believed to be associated with it.

Early in 1965, the New York City school system, the largest in the nation, experienced one of several such boycotts directed against it. The boycott, termed "Operation Shutdown," popularly known as the " '600' School Boycott," was planned and sponsored by the Citywide Committee for Integrated Education, led by the Rev. Milton A. Galamison, pastor of the Siloam Presbyterian Church of Brooklyn, and the

Harlem Parents Committee, a group organized to fight for school integration.

This move was rooted in the belief that immediate desegregation of the New York City public schools was possible. Operation Shutdown reflected the feeling that unless something were done quickly to break the pattern of *de facto* segregated schooling, seen as inherently inferior, another generation of Negro youth would be left far behind in the race for equality in America. Believing that only militant action would make the New York Board of Education produce a specific program aimed at integrating the schools, the leaders planned a long-range school shutdown. This appeared to them to be the best technique available to impress upon the civil authorities their urgent demand that stringent efforts be made to desegregate city schools.

As their target, the sponsors hoped to close thirty-one *de facto* segregated junior high schools (those schools with populations of 90 per cent or more Negroes and Puerto Ricans), as well as the seven "600" day schools of the city (schools for children with emotional or behavioral maladjustments). They aimed at reaching their target by February 3, 1965.

Specifically, they called for the appointment of 200 Negro and Puerto Rican teachers to supervisory positions; immediate desegregation of the thirty-one *de facto* segregated junior high schools; a change in the 1965-1966 construction program with a deliberate effort to locate schools in such a way as to facilitate integrated student bodies; a reevaluation of all the "600" schools; and a plan and timetable for the desegregation of all schools.

THE HISTORICAL BACKGROUND

Early Approaches

Operation Shutdown was one of several boycotts that had been directed against the New York City school system.

When the United States Supreme Court in 1954 declared school segregation unconstitutional[1] after nearly three-quarters of a century of legally sanctioned segregation, many New Yorkers approved this, resting comfortably in the knowledge that segregation by race had been outlawed in their school system since 1902. They were, therefore, quite surprised by accusations that, despite the fact that segregation was not sanctioned by law, it was in effect sanctioned by custom, for the pattern of Negro housing and the concept of the neighborhood school, which required that children attend the school located in the district in which they lived, had created a segregated school system, particularly at the elementary- and junior-high-school levels.

In addition, it was becoming increasingly clear to civil-rights groups that the *de facto* segregated schools of the city were not providing minority-group children in such major residential areas as Harlem and Bedford-Stuyvesant with the kind of education that would enable them to take their places in the economic and social life of this nation on an equal competitive basis with others. Under the most ideal conditions of equality in education, any compulsory attendance requirements would be resisted by some unable or unwilling, for a variety of reasons, to be subject to its constraints. Where conditions of equality did not exist, however, civil-rights groups maintained that compulsory attendance at what were regarded as inferior schools was, in effect, deliberate denial of constitutional rights.

At first the officials of the Board of Education maintained the position that *de facto* segregated schools were not discriminatory or inferior and did not violate the mandate set forth by the Supreme Court decision of 1954. The legality of this position was soon tested. Tentative first steps in this direction came from individuals who sought to register their children in schools outside their neighborhoods. Unsuccess-

[1] *Brown v. Board of Education, 1954.*

ful in their efforts, several parents then tested the legality
of the compulsory-attendance law by keeping their children
out of the *de facto* segregated schools to which they were
assigned.

These cases came to be popularly known as the "Harlem
Nine," and as a result of this small-scale boycott came a
highly significant decision by Justice Justine W. Polier, in
1958.[2] Dismissing the charges brought by the Board of Education against two of the parents, she argued that the
court could not enforce the unconstitutional denial of constitutional rights. Her decision led to the institution of plans
by the Board of Education that allowed parents to apply
for the voluntary transfer of their children outside their
neighborhoods, when the schools there were considered inferior, to schools elsewhere that had space for them.

At first, Open Enrollment, as this plan became known,
was widely hailed as an integration effort. It soon became
clear to civil-rights groups, however, that this was not an
adequate answer to their demands for improved education,
which they viewed as inseparably tied to integrated education. Voluntary plans were not seen as effective, for they
resulted in little more than the voluntary busing of limited
numbers of children. The reasons for this varied from the
desire of parents to keep young children near home to suspicion concerning their treatment in schools receiving them
to resentment of the fact that only Negro children would
be moved. Inertia and apathy on the part of the school system in relation to integration efforts were also factors to be
considered. In addition, the burden of effort rested on parents, many of whom were unaccustomed to coping with
bureaucratic procedures. Therefore, civil-rights groups believed that any substantial plan must eliminate the voluntary
aspect.

[2] In the Matter of Charlene Skipworth and Another, 14 *Miscellaneous
Reports*, 2nd Series (Albany, N.Y.: Williams Press, 1959), pp. 325-347.

By 1960, the Board of Education of New York City had officially endorsed the principle of integrated education for its system.[3] Several reports and plans to that effect were issued.[4] However, these plans, still voluntary, were not viewed as bold enough approaches to the problem, and pressures from the civil-rights movement for deliberate programs to desegregate the schools began to mount.

On January 29, 1964, the Board of Education issued a new, eagerly awaited plan.[5] This plan, entitled "Better Education through Integration," endorsed the principle that quality education and integration were related. It pointed out that the problems of *de facto* segregation were related to problems of housing and employment. However, the report laid down few timetables for achieving better racial balance in the schools, thereby evoking the bitter disappointment of those civil-rights groups that were impatient for action.

School Boycott 1964

Thus, on February 3, 1964, one week after the issuance of the report, an unprecedented one-day boycott of the New York City public schools took place. School authorities said that 464,361 pupils, or 44.8 per cent of the total enrollment of over a million youngsters, were absent. With the normal absentee rate being 100,000, the tremendous success of the boycott was evident.

The 1964 boycott was widely supported by civil-rights organizations: the Congress of Racial Equality (CORE), the

[3] *Toward Greater Opportunity*, Board of Education, City of New York, June 1960.
[4] *Progress Toward Integration Sept. 1—Nov. 30, 1963 and Plans for the Immediate Future*, Interim Report December 1963, Board of Education, City of New York; and *Plan for Integration*, Board of Education, City of New York, August 23, 1963.
[5] *Better Education through Integration*, Board of Education, City of New York, January 29, 1964.

National Association for the Advancement of Colored People (NAACP), the Urban League of Greater New York, the National Association for Puerto Rican Civil Rights, and many local groups. Large numbers of clergymen and many city teachers joined in the demonstration. Bayard Rustin, who had led the March on Washington the previous summer, James Farmer, Rev. Milton Galamison, and Thelma Johnson took active leadership roles.

The leaders were jubilant at the response to their call for a boycott of the city's schools. Bayard Rustin, for example, stated:

> I think we are on the threshold of a new political movement—and I do not mean it in the party sense—that is going to change the face of New York in housing, in jobs, and in schools. . . . Winds of discontent are about to sweep over the city . . .

> The boycott and the rent strike are fair warning that the civil rights revolution has reached out of the South and is now knocking at our own doors.[6]

Several features distinguished the February 3, 1964, boycott. First was the expression of unity between the many groups working on the matter of civil rights. Second was the participation of the Puerto Rican community. Third was the tremendous numbers of people who supported the tactic, as attested by the official Board of Education attendance figures. Those school districts with predominantly Negro and Puerto Rican populations showed the highest rate of absence. Fourth was the orderly, peaceful nature of the demonstrations involved. Despite 20-degree weather, pickets marched at 300 of the city's 860 public schools. Three thousand five hundred demonstrators, most of them children, but with a large number of adults participating, marched on Board of Education headquarters in an orderly, spirited demonstration. In the face of this remarkable display of

[6] *New York Times*, February 4, 1964.

united dissatisfaction with the educational system of New York City, the President of the Board of Education, James B. Donovan, said:

> All these people proved is how easy it is to get children to take a holiday instead of going to school. They also showed that parents could be frightened into keeping their children at home by a campaign of intimidation and threats of possible violence.[7]

Mr. Donovan summed up his view of the boycott by calling it a "fizzle."

James Farmer, then National Director of CORE, retorted:

"My God, what a flop; what a fizzle! We need more fizzles like this!"

Cheering, youthful demonstrators were dispersed in orderly fashion by leaders who warned that violence was what the Board wanted. Bayard Rustin, for example, told his listeners that they would succeed in severely disappointing Mr. Donovan by dispersing peacefully.

One bystander was reported as saying:

"I can't understand what these people want. They have more freedom in our city than anywhere else. When I went to school they didn't allow such nonsense."[8]

The demonstration had been called to protest the Board of Education's integration plan, announced the previous week and regarded as inadequate. The civil-rights groups were pressing for more rapid racial integration of all schools in the city. They believed their show of strength would quicken the pace of change in the New York City schools.

The Search for Solutions—The Allen Report

As a result of the one-day boycott in 1964, the city turned to State Education Commissioner Allen for help in developing a plan for integrating the New York City school system.

[7] *New York Times*, February 4, 1964.
[8] *Ibid.*

Meanwhile the pressures from the civil-rights movement were met by countermoves on the part of those white parents who reacted with alarm to the possibility of an end coming to the neighborhood-school concept. The following March, one month after the civil-rights boycott, Parents and Taxpayers (PAT) and the Joint Council for Better Education, white citizens' groups, picketed City Hall and called on the Mayor to prevent the Board from carrying out its announced plan of pairing several schools for purposes of achieving improved racial balance.

Although the February 3 boycott had held out much hope that action would be taken rapidly to ensure desegregation of *de facto* segregated schools, it became apparent to civil-rights groups that the counterpressures from PAT, plus the inertia of the vast bureaucratic school system, were operating to stall or inhibit large-scale changes. Thus, in March, the Citywide Committee for Integrated Schools called another one-day boycott. This time, 270,000 pupils were absent, a drop of nearly 200,000 below that of the earlier boycott, but an impressive number nonetheless. Part of the explanation for this drop rested on the fact that several organizations, among them the NAACP, were awaiting the publication of the Board of Education's plans and hence did not actively take part.

On May 12, 1964, the long awaited Allen Report was issued.[9] Prepared by John H. Fischer, President of Teachers College, Columbia University; Kenneth Clark, the noted psychologist; and Rabbi Judah Cahn, with the assistance of the Institute of Urban Studies, Teachers College, headed by Robert Dentler, the report documented in detail the growth of *de facto* segregation in New York City. The report recognized that this was the result of shifts in population

[9] *Desegregating the Public Schools of New York City,* a report prepared for the Board of Education of the City of New York by the State Education Commissioner's Advisory Committee on Human Relations and Community Tension, 1964.

in the city and noted that no program to slow the trend toward segregation could be effective without tremendously increased financial aid to the city schools by the city, state, and federal governments. Several concrete recommendations were made:

1. Comprehensive four year high schools should be built at points well outside existing ethnic ghettoes, to be attended by commuting youths from points all over the city as well as by local residents.
2. Fifth through eighth-grade middle schools should replace junior high schools ultimately in the entire system. The purpose of these units should be to furnish improved instruction for older children. They should be so located as to provide for as many children as possible an experience in an integrated school. Shuttle buses should be used to reach these middle schools.
3. Primary units extending from pre-kindergarten classes through the fourth grade should replace existing elementary schools. These units would still be neighborhood schools, but they would be organized differently and would feed into the middle schools. Many existing elementary schools could be reorganized to contain two or more primary units.
4. *Educational complexes* should be formed, consisting of from two to six primary units clustered around the middle schools. These should be managed by a single administrator, with assistant administrators in the separate unit buildings. The *complexes* should integrate educational activities, improve the distribution of facilities and resources, and promote communication between faculties, parents, and students from diverse ethnic backgrounds. *Complexes* should have a high degree of organizational autonomy over their programs.
5. Eventually, educational parks housed in newly developed structures on cleared sites should replace single middle schools with their *educational complexes*.
6. Facilities should be equalized in every way, so that

mainly Puerto Rican and Negro schools in the city will *not* continue to be older, more overcrowded, and in greater need of installation of essential facilities than other schools.

7. The new organization of the system should be utilized to stabilize and improve the staffing of the schools. The middle schools and clustered primary units with their new autonomy should be used to attract and retain the best teachers and administrators.

8. Board programs to improve recruitment and advancement of minority group teachers and other personnel should be extended and intensified. As part of this, training relations between the system and local teacher training institutions must be greatly strengthened.

9. Pre-primary programs of instruction should be introduced on a city-wide basis, serving children as young as three years.

10. Special schools and programs, particularly those for maladjusted and retarded students, should be studied independently and the findings should be made public. A stronger policy for retaining more such students in their regular schools should be pursued.

11. State and Federal support, fiscal and administrative, should be provided to the city to accomplish these necessary changes. This support should begin after the Board of Education has demonstrated its new initiative and commitment by taking some of the steps toward desegregation which do not involve additional municipal expenditures.

Our proposals do, we trust, make plain the fact that substantial forces must be reckoned with and redirected if desegregation is to be achieved. If these proposals are adopted and implemented we are confident they will effect some immediate desgregation. More importantly, they would help prevent an increase in the rate of segregation within the schools. To accomplish this, however, they would have to be introduced promptly, progressively, and in an ever more extensive network during the next five years.[10]

The Allen Commission's Report was greeted with acclaim by the civil-rights movement, but as the months passed and a new school year approached, no specific plans for the implementation of the Allen Report were forthcoming. Disappointment and apprehension concerning the slowness of the Board in producing concrete plans began to mount.

Counterpressures

In addition, countermoves by white groups opposing the efforts to pair schools and bus children began to gain in strength. When school opened in September, a new boycott took place, this time led by the white group, PAT, protesting the school-pairing plans which were coming into effect on a trial basis. In this demonstration, 275,638 pupils, representing a total of 175,000 over normal absentees, were out of school. This boycott had been called in an effort to insure the continuation of the neighborhood school and attracted those white parents who vociferously opposed the transfer of their children outside the immediate neighborhoods in which they lived. Although ordinarily all parents, white and Negro, prefer young children to be close to home, this protest on the part of white citizens' groups became identified as antagonistic to Negroes' demands for new types of school organization to break the pattern of *de facto* segregation.

As the year closed, the promise of change given by the tremendous show of strength on February 4, 1964, had not been fulfilled. Impatient and distrustful of the delay, Reverend Galamison put Operation Shutdown into effect. He hoped that Operation Shutdown would cause the Board of Education to move more quickly in the direction of implementing the Allen Report.

[10] *Ibid.,* pp. 28-30.

OPERATION SHUTDOWN

The Event

On the night of January 16, 1965, a twenty-four hour "Vigil of Intervention" was held by Equal, a white parents group which supported integration efforts. Ellen Lurie, Chairman of Equal, had announced this activity in support of school desegregation and in the hope that Reverend Galamison's demands would be met without resorting to a school boycott. The Harlem Parents Committee supported the vigil and urged all its members and friends to participate.

Although it succeeded in attracting publicity, the vigil did not succeed in calling forth any immediate changes in school organization. And so plans for shutting down thirty-one *de facto* segregated junior high schools, as well as the city's "600" schools, proceeded. On January 19, 1965, the first school was shut down by Reverend Galamison. One hundred and thirty-six students stayed out of a Brooklyn "600" school, the total enrollment of which was 150. Twenty adult pickets appeared before the school carrying placards that read, "SORRY—THIS SCHOOL IS CLOSED," and " '600' SCHOOLS DO NOT EDUCATE."

At one junior high school in the heart of Bedford-Stuyvesant, Brooklyn, an almost all-Negro area, the president of the Parents Association, himself a Negro, shouted to the children: "Let's go to school, children. This is where we get an education, not in the streets. If you want something, you stay inside the school and fight for it."

A mother shouted: "They have everything we need in that school. It's up to us to get it."

In answer to these and other admonitions to attend school, pickets shouted: "Don't go to school today, boys. This school died of segregation."

Others shouted: "This school is closed. Go to a freedom school."

Nearly 700 of this particular school's population of close to 1,700 did not cross the picket lines to enter school. The picket line included white students from schools throughout the borough. Their assistance was welcomed by Reverend Galamison despite taunts from the Parents Association president that these were not community people nor would they want to live in the community.

The Board of Education moved quickly to stop the action through the courts. State Supreme Court Justice M. Henry Martuscello signed a temporary injunction against the boycott, and plans were made by the Board of Education to have Galamison arrested for violation of Section 5a of State Education Law 3212 which reads:

> No person shall induce a minor to absent himself from attendance upon required instruction or harbor him while he is absent or aid and abet him in violating any provision of part one of this article.[11]

In response to this action, the New York Civil Liberties Union called the injunction issued by the courts ". . . an outrageous effort to cut off Freedom of Speech and Assembly."[12] The organization charged the Board of Education with attempting to silence the criticism of private citizens with respect to public policies.

The shutdown was a scant two days old when Reverend Galamison and Thelma Johnson, a leader of the Harlem Parents Committee, were arrested but quickly released on a temporary writ of reasonable doubt.[13] The boycott soon began to pick up momentum and spread to *de facto* segre-

[11] McKinney's Consolidated Laws of New York, Annotated, Book 16, Education Law Part 2 (Brooklyn, N.Y., Edward Thompson Co., 1953), p. 348.
[12] *New York Times,* January 22, 1965.
[13] Isaiah Robinson became spokesman for the Harlem Parents Committee after Mrs. Johnson's arrest.

gated junior high schools. By February 4, 1965, there were some 6,000 absences, 2,000 above normal, out of a school population of 55,000 attending the schools affected by the shutdown. Although the original target of closing all thirty-one *de facto* segregated junior high schools and the "600" schools had not been met, fourteen junior high schools and three "600" schools were affected.

Reactions to Operation Shutdown

Almost without exception, the press, civil authorities, and the educational system condemned Operation Shutdown. James B. Donovan, President of the Board of Education, termed the boycott a "reprehensible act." Dr. Calvin E. Gross, then Superintendent of Schools, called the boycott "a conscienceless use of children by adults who ought to be working with other adults, not using children." Police Commissioner Michael J. Murphy questioned "the wisdom of those who encourage this kind of activity in which children are being used as pawns."[14]

Within the schools themselves, few staff members rallied to Galamison's support. The teachers did not participate in the shutdown, something that some of them had done in previous school boycotts. Those opposed to this shutdown for reasons other than questions of tactics and timing considered Galamison a demagogue, a rabble-rouser, one who appealed to "hysterical elements," and an inciter to school chaos. His effect on children was believed by many to be developing hostility toward school, teachers, and whites, thus hampering the school in its positive efforts to help children. These educators interpreted the behavior of boycotting pupils as arrogant and hostile toward authority. This behavior was seen as emanating from the propaganda of the boycott leaders.

[14] *New York Times,* February 24, 1965.

The boycott of a "600" school brought forth strong criticism from the press. The *New York Times* editorial page of January 21, 1965, read:

Boycotting a "600" School

The boycott of Public School 617 in Brooklyn is an act of unpardonable irresponsibility. The Rev. Milton A. Galamison, who organized the action, cannot plead ignorance of the human and educational harm he has done in asking 136 students—many of them emotionally disturbed, some retarded, and others chronic truants and discipline cases—to stay out of school. The use of pupils as pawns in a boycott is detrimental even to ordinary children; in this case it is nothing short of criminal.

There are serious flaws in the concept and operation of the "600" schools, as there are in the general treatment of children needing psychological attention in this understaffed and inadequately financed system. This is not an integration issue. All hands and all minds are needed to find better answers. But needed also is the humility to admit that there are vast areas of human need which cannot be solved by polemics and aimless militancy. Least of all can they be solved by telling children already deep in trouble that they can serve a cause by breaking the law.

When several hundred Negro teen-agers were involved in a near-riot situation in the streets of downtown Brooklyn, the fears of those who opposed Reverend Galamison's call for a boycott seemed to be realized.

The national civil-rights organizations did not participate in the boycott, although, as it neared its close, James Farmer, national president of CORE, declared his support. In answer to the criticism concerning the involvement of children in protest activity he said:

We reject the idea that children should not be used in school shutdowns. Children are involved in the integration struggle in the South, and they should be involved in it in

THE CLERGY COMMITTED FOR BETTER SCHOOLS is an ecumenical and interracial action group to work for quality integrated education.

This group will utilize all responsible means, including non-violent civil disobedience, to alert the City to the injustice of segregated schools and to the ways in which this injustice can be corrected.

The demand of this group is that the Board of Education issue, and make a public commitment to, a City-wide plan and timetable for school desegregation in accordance with the Allen Report of May 12, 1964.

The Clergy Committed for Better Schools invites the participation of all priests, pastors, ministers and rabbis in its program of action.

"Clergy Committed for Better Schools"
1121 Bedford Ave.
Brooklyn 16, NY

No longer will the clergy of New York be used as puppets, popping up and down with invocations and benedictions to place a halo around the unjust status quo.

The clergyman also has a divine call to censure and condemn injustice. We cannot sanction by silence an evil that is abhorrent to God and abhorrent to God-fearing men.

New York's segregated school system is such an injustice and evil. Hundreds of thousands of children are being cheated of an equal educational opportunity. Segregated ghetto schools are graduating functional illiterates who cannot pass even the minimal tests to enter military service. A whole generation of Negroes and Puerto Ricans are being educated for a lifetime on Welfare or to compete for jobs as porters and broom pushers. It is cruel to instill in these children high hopes for college education when, by the time they reach Junior High, they are already more than three years behind their white counterparts.

The cruel injustice of segregated schools will not be resolved by another crash program. We will not be deceived by the euphemisms of "Operation More" or "Higher Horizons." We hold with the Supreme Court of the United States that separate education never has been and never can be equal education.

We do not ask for miracles. Desegregation of the schools may take 5, 10, or even 15 years. Desegregation should be orderly but definite.

FACSIMILE OF A PORTION OF AN APPEAL FOR SCHOOL INTEGRATION.

the North. They suffer segregation and discrimination as much as their elders.[15]

The national civil-rights groups at that time were concentrating on voter-registration drives in the South. The civil-rights movement in general had been moving in the direction of less direct activist confrontation with discrimination and in the direction of voter registration and voter education. It was working to increase the political participation of previously inactive Negroes, now that most of the legal barriers to equality had been removed by the Civil Rights Act of 1964.

But Reverend Galamison was not without support. Among the staunchest of his supporters were members of the ministry. In a pastoral letter to the Presbytery of New York City, the Rev. G. E. McClellan, General Presbyter, wrote:

> The Negroes and the Puerto Ricans have had it, and Mr. Galamison dramatically represents that fact. The people he leads are not out to win our favor and approbation but to win educational rights for their children.

The letter added:

> They have waited for the rest of us to respond to the shocking studies, to exhibit concern for the full education of all children. They have complained, they have pleaded. And basically, we have done nothing.

Seventy clergymen termed Galamison's arrest as "anti-Negro and anti-Protestant." The Rev. Dr. Gardner C. Taylor wrote:

> Since no action seems strong enough to persuade the Board of Education to integrate the city's schools, other than that being led by the Citywide Committee for Inte-

[15] Speech delivered at City College of the City University of New York, February 25, 1965.

grated Schools, we are left with no alternative but to pledge our influence and support to this imaginative and necessary effort.

The Protestant Council of the City of New York also expressed its respect and its sympathy for the cause that the leaders of the shutdown represented.

Support for the shutdown came from the parents associated with the Citywide Committee for Integrated Schools and the Harlem Parents Committee. Some parents, less militant than Galamison's followers but committed to the national civil-rights movement, kept their children out of school for one or two days in token evidence of their support for integration and improved schooling but then insisted that the children return to school, frequently escorting them into the buildings.

Despite the efforts of its leaders, the shutdown did not succeed in attracting large numbers of unorganized Negro adults. Also, parents' associations in *de facto* segregated schools did not officially support the shutdown, nor did the white parents in Equal who had called the Vigil of Intervention. However, individual white parents who belonged to Equal prepared and donated package lunches for the children attending freedom schools.

The greatest support for the shutdown came from the children who absented themselves from school and instead attended freedom schools. Some of these youngsters, previously uncommitted to the civil-rights movement, emerged as leaders. Not all were the children of parents committed to the boycott movement. Parents sometimes did not know their children were involved. Some parents did not themselves participate but considered that if their children wished to they could.

The youngsters wrote songs, leaflets, and picket signs. They organized around picket captains chosen from their ranks, ran mimeograph machines, and distributed leaflets.

To Parents Who Say, No "SHUTDOWN"

1. What means more to you your kids or your P.T.A. President?

2. What are your children learning in school?

3. Do you believe there is but one race, the human race?

4. If answer to question 3 is yes, why do you say no SHUTDOWN and all SHUTDOWN means is to integrate our schools and give your child an equal education?

5. Do you have a carefree conscience? If so, ask yourself this question. Would you give your child rat poison just because he did not go to bed on time?

6. If answer to question 5 is no, why do you tell your child to go to school during a period of SHUTDOWN, and violate the basic principles of respect to a picket line? And their race, you are killing them little by little and destroying their mind.

FACT:

IF YOU BELIEVE IN:

1. Martin Luther King, Jr. and his Dream.

2. Milton Galamison and his City-Wide Committee for Integrated Schools.

3. Brooklyn CORE

4. Fighters of Macon

5. And above all, your child - give her or him an EQUAL EDUCATION. KEEP HIM OUT OF SCHOOL DURING THE PERIOD OF SHUTDOWN AND SEND THEM TO FREEDOM SCHOOLS.

RETURN TO:

FIGHTERS OF MACON
260 Jefferson Avenue
Brooklyn, New York 11216

FACSIMILE OF LEAFLET DISTRIBUTED DURING OPERATION SHUTDOWN, FEBRUARY—MARCH, 1965.

As noted, those who attended freedom schools became leaders of the shutdown, the movement depending primarily on the boys and girls themselves.

With limited organizational support, the shutdown did not achieve its original target. However, it did last seven weeks and at its height kept approximately 6,000 youngsters out of 55,000 from attending school.

SUMMARY

Operation Shutdown, 1965, was one of a series of dramatic, active protests directed against the educational system on the part of urban Negroes living in our inner cities. Not only in New York, but also in other cities throughout the North, such boycotts are becoming common.

Educators, traditionally committed to the school system as providing equal opportunity to all, according to their abilities, have frequently been both surprised and angered by the accusations that they are prejudiced against Negroes and that their schools provide unequal educational opportunities for Negro youth. Those in financially hard-pressed urban school systems have been particularly angered by the use of a method, school absence, that results in the loss of needed state revenues. For the educator it seems "natural" that school-attendance laws should be obeyed and that if there are serious complaints about the school system they should be presented through the appropriate bureaucratic channels.

To the educator, anyone who would deliberately keep his child out of school or involve children in protesting against the educational system seems strange, if not reprehensible. Yet, there is nothing "natural" about attendance laws or the expression of social protest solely through bureaucratic channels or the courts. In Latin America and European countries, for example, students often engage in street demonstrations against educators and government. In our own country, student protests have increasingly appeared in universities, extending from the University of California at Berkeley on the West Coast to staid Yale in the East. The strike and the boycott have long been the weapons of protest. That they are now being applied to education comes as a surprise to many, particularly as they involve children of compulsory-school-attendance age.

To understand school boycotts, and particularly Operation Shutdown, we must consider the consequences of the modern educational system for the Negro children of the inner city, as well as the role of the boycott in training the Negro for an active concern with formal education and active participation in the acceptable channels for vertical mobility in our society.

2. BACKGROUND TO CONFLICT

IN AMERICA, education offered by the public schools has been seen as providing the tools with which immigrants and newcomers to urban areas have been able to move from the slums into more prestigious and remunerative positions in the larger society. Public education in this country is presumed to operate as a training ground for vertical mobility in American economic and political life.

Yet, for many Negro youths, the educational system has failed to perform the function of providing the transition between slum life and meaningful roles in the larger society. In the years since the United States Supreme Court outlawed *de jure* segregation, there has been mounting evidence that the inner-city schools have not been achieving the goals of education for Negro youth.[1] The inner-city

[1] Patricia A. Sexton, *Education and Income* (New York: Viking Press, 1961); *Youth in the Ghetto* (New York: Harlem Youth Opportunities Unlimited, 1964), pp. 161-244; *The Status of Public School Education of Negro and Puerto Rican Children in New York City* (New York: New York Public

schools, subjected to critical analysis by increasingly concerned civil-rights leaders and social scientists, were revealed as providing substandard staff, facilities, and pupil performance.

EDUCATIONAL FAILURE IN THE CITY

Although the problem of substandard education in the inner-city schools was not confined to New York City, it was there that an exhaustive study of the Harlem school dramatically documented the dismal picture as it applied to minority youth.[2] The HARYOU Report pointed to the fact that, although Harlem youngsters started at a par with the nation at third grade, after this grade achievement levels were progressively behind both the city and nation. In third grade, central Harlem pupils were fully one year behind the achievement levels of New York City pupils. By the sixth grade they had fallen nearly two years behind, and by the eighth grade they were about two and one-half years behind.[3] These conclusions were not based on longitudinal studies and must be interpreted cautiously. They do, however, attest to the massive educational failure for many children evident in these schools. Concerning the prospects for these children, the report states:

Less than half of Central Harlem's youth seems destined to complete High School, and of those that do, most will

Education Association, 1955); James B. Conant, *Slums and Suburbs* (New York: McGraw-Hill Book Company, Inc., 1961); Robert J. Havighurst, *The Public Schools of Chicago* (Chicago: Board of Education, 1964); Max Wolff, *A Study of Racial Imbalance in the Plainfield Public Schools* (Plainfield, N.J.: Board of Education, 1962); and Martin Deutsch, *Minority Groups and Class Status as Related to Social and Educational Factors in Scholastic Achievement*, Monograph No. 2, Society for Applied Anthropology, 1960.

[2] *Youth in the Ghetto* (commonly known as The HARYOU Report).

[3] *Ibid.*, p. 194.

JIM CROW SCHOOLS

Shame of the City!!!!

THE BEDFORD. STUYVESANT SCHOOLS

Six Reasons Why the 31 Segregated Junior High Schools Should
Be Shut-down until the Board of Education Gives a Plan and
Timetable for the Desegregation of New York City Public Schools
Which Will Provide Equal Education for All Children.

* * * * * * * * * * * * * * *

1. The program is very poor.

2. The schools have the most INEXPERIENCED TEACHERS.

3. Because the children ARE NEGRO and PUERTO RICAN the
   teachers DO NOT expect them to learn.

4. The attitude of many of THE TEACHERS is prejudiced.

5. The children are 2 to 3 years BEHIND in reading.

6. There is NOTHING in the textbooks that relates to the
   Negro and Puerto Rican child and constructively identi-
   fies them with American history and culture.

ACT NOW!!   TARGET DATE   Feb. 3, 1965

Don't be afraid to use every possible means to protect

your child against ignorance and poverty.

Citywide Committee for Integrated Schools, 270 Jefferson Avenue,
Brooklyn, New York

Milton A. Galamison   Brooklyn CORE

FACSIMILE OF LEAFLET DISTRIBUTED DURING OPERATION
SHUTDOWN, FEBRUARY–MARCH, 1965.

join the ranks of those with no vocational skills, no developed talents, and consequently, little or no future.[4]

Although no comparable study has been made of the large concentration of Negro youths in the Bedford-Stuyvesant and Brownsville sections of Brooklyn, the levels of achievement are generally believed to be little different.

The failure of the schools to provide the skills for vertical mobility is widespread and evident in many situations. Without the academic tools for further formal learning, many Negro youths are cut off early in their lives from the route by which higher economic positions are achieved by other Americans.

REASONS FOR FAILURE

Many arguments are concerned with determining the responsibility for this failure. Generally they revolve about three major factors. The first is the genetic, which deals with racial factors or individual intelligence factors. Science had not accepted the racial explanation.[5] Intelligence may

---

[4] *Ibid.*, p. 188.

[5] See Otto Klineberg, "Negro-White Differences in Intelligence Test Performance: A New Look at an Old Problem," *American Psychologist*. Vol. 4 (April 1965), 198-203; and Thomas F. Pettigrew, "Negro American Intelligence: A New Look at an Old Controversy," *Journal of Negro Education*, Vol. 33 No. 1 (Winter 1964).

Various scientific organizations have made official statements concerning this issue: "There are differences in intelligence test scores when one compares a random sample of whites and Negroes. What is equally clear is that no evidence exists that leads to the conclusion that such differences are innate. Quite to the contrary, the evidence points overwhelmingly to the fact that when one compares Negroes and whites of comparable cultural and educational background, differences in intelligence diminish markedly; the more comparable the background, the less the difference. There is no direct evidence that supports the view that there is an innate difference between members of different racial groups . . . We regret that Professor Garrett feels that his colleagues are foisting an 'equalitarian dogma' on the public. There is no question of dogma involved. Evidence speaks for itself

explain individual success or failure but cannot explain the widespread failure evident in our schools.

The second argument revolves about problems of social deprivation, poverty, slum culture, lack of motivation, and various other factors that have come to characterize descriptions of the "culturally deprived." Although these explanations are appealing, they may be deceptive. They have been questioned by Kenneth Clark, who asks:

> To what extent are the contemporary social deprivation theories merely substituting notions of environmental immutability and fatalism for earlier notions of biologically determined educational unmodifiability? To what extent do these theories obscure more basic reasons for the educational retardation of lower-status children? To what extent do they offer acceptable and desired alibis for the educational default: the fact that these children, by and large, do not learn because they are not being taught effectively and they are not being taught because those who are

and it casts serious doubt on the conclusion that there is any innate inequality in intelligence in different racial groups . . ." (The Society for the Psychological Study of Social Issues, a division of the American Psychological Association, 1961); ". . . The great preponderance of scientific opinion has favored the conclusion that there is little or no ground on which to assume that the racial groups in question are innately different in any important human capacity . . . The conclusion of scientists is that the differences in test performance by members of so-called racial groups are due not to racial but to environmental factors. This is the operating assumption today of the vast majority of the competent scientists in the field . . ." (The Society for the Study of Social Problems, a section of the American Sociological Association, 1961); "The American Anthropological Association repudiates statements now appearing in the United States that Negroes are biologically and in innate mental ability inferior to whites, and reaffirms the fact that there is no scientifically established evidence to justify the exclusion of any race from the rights guaranteed by the constitution of the United States. The basic principles of equality of opportunity and equality before the law are compatible with all that is known about human biology. All races possess the abilities needed to participate fully in the democratic way of life and in modern technological civilization." (American Anthropological Association, resolution passed by a unanimous 192 to 0 vote, 1961)

charged with the responsibility of teaching them do not believe that they can learn, do not expect that they can learn, and do not act toward them in ways which help them to learn.[6]

In his questions, Professor Clark has suggested the third factor that involves the failure of the schools themselves to provide adequate educational facilities and programs for the children of the inner city.

Certainly, for any individual, any factor or a combination of factors may explain educational deficiency. However, the massive failure evident in the *de facto* segregated schools of New York City is considered by the HARYOU Report as the responsibility of the schools themselves. The report states:

> On the evidence available to date, it must be concluded that the major reason why an increasing number of Central Harlem pupils fall below their grade levels is that *substandard performance is expected of them.*[7]

As a result of the deteriorating conditions in these schools, "schools have lost faith in the ability of their pupils to learn, and the community has lost faith in the ability of the schools to teach."[8]

Increasingly, to the leaders of civil-rights movements, *de facto* segregated schools have been viewed as providing inferior education for Negro youths and denying them access to mobility in American life. The great promise of "freedom now," that is, full equality in a prosperous America, was being frustrated by a school system viewed as providing inferior teaching facilities for Negro youths, a milieu of hopelessness and increased separation of Negro slum youths from the larger society. In order to encourage breaking out

[6] Kenneth B. Clark, *Dark Ghetto* (New York: Harper & Row), p. 131.
[7] *Youth in the Ghetto*, p. 237.
[8] *Ibid.*, p. 236.

of this ring of despair, a whole series of attacks were launched on *de facto* segregation.

The New York City Board of Education, too, recognized the need to do something about the dismal levels of educational attainment in the *de facto* segregated schools. They launched a series of special programs, among them Higher Horizons and the More Effective Schools program, designed to raise educational levels by improving facilities in such schools.[9]

By the more militant groups, like the Harlem Parents Committee, programs designed by the Board of Education to improve the education in these schools were viewed with disdain as measures designed to circumvent integration.

Others, recognizing the tremendous difficulty inherent in effecting desegregation given the vast populations involved, argued that *de facto* segregated schools could be improved.

A number of individuals prominent in the civil rights movement claim, however, that a demand for excellence in ghetto schools is really camouflage for acquiescence in segregation. On the contrary it is, given the intransigence of the white community and the impossibilty of immediate integration, a decision to save as many Negro children as possible now. The struggle of the civil rights groups for a better life for these children is made more difficult, if not impossible, if the methods of the struggle become dominated by inflexible emotional postures. Heroics and dramatic words and gestures, over-simplified either-or thinking, and devil-hunting might dominate headlines; but they cannot solve the fundamental problem of obtaining high-quality education in the public schools and the related problem of realistic and serious desegregation of

[9] At first these programs seemed highly successful. Hailed by many as a solution, they were criticized by others as merely creating a placebo effect. Recent evidence indicates that the success of these programs, particularly Higher Horizons, is open to question.

these schools. These children, Negro or white, must not be sacrificed on the altar of ideological and semantic rigidities.[10]

Despite their disagreements over tactics and solutions, however, all Negro leaders are concerned about the failure of the schools to educate Negro youths effectively.

THE SIGNIFICANCE OF FAILURE

The consequences of the failure of the urban schools to prepare lower-status youth successfully for equal participation in the larger society cannot be understood without reference to the total involvement of the problem with major social and economic changes occurring in this country.

Perhaps the most significant of these changes is the accelerated application of industrial techniques to agricultural practice, leading to the tremendous outpouring of millions of farmer-owners, tenants, and laborers from the rural areas of the nation to the cities. All rural Americans have been affected, but, for Negroes, the change has been particularly dramatic. In 1940, 49 per cent of the Negro population was classified as urban. By 1960, this figure had risen to 73 per cent—higher than comparable figures for whites.[11] During the past twenty years alone, 3 million Negroes have moved to the cities of the North, swelling the size of the Negro population of New York City to 1.3 million, of Chicago, to 900,000, of Philadelphia and Detroit to over .5 million each, and increasing the Negro population of Los Angeles over 600 per cent.[12] Although some of this popula-

---

[10] Clark, *op. cit.*, pp. 117-118.

[11] Karl E. Taeuber and Alma F. Taeuber, *Negroes in Cities: Residential Segregation and Neighborhood Change* (Chicago: Aldine Publishing Co., 1965), p. 143.

[12] Charles E. Silberman, *Crisis in Black and White* (New York: Random House, 1964), pp. 30-31.

tion is rural in origin, many Negro migrants to northern cities are from other metropolitan regions and represent a population of rising social and economic status.[13]

Like earlier generations of migrants, the Negro tended to live in the older sections of the inner city. At the same time, the expanding suburbs of post-World-War-II America were absorbing the vast numbers of whites who left the city. As a result, the urban Negro found himself as effectively segregated by housing patterns in the northern city as he had been in the South by *de jure* discrimination. Even economic prosperity for those able to move into the middle class did not mean easy access to housing outside the residential ghetto.[14]

Although the cities of the North in the past were able to absorb and integrate the millions of migrants arriving from Europe at an earlier period, the Negro and white of today have arrived at a time when accelerated automation is rapidly wiping out the jobs that unskilled newcomers to the city have ordinarily filled.

This problem is recognized by the federal government. Secretary of Labor Wirtz has pointed out:

> The confluence of surging labor population and driving technology is splitting the American labor force into tens of millions of "haves" and millions of "have-nots." In our economy of 69,000,000 jobs, those with wanted skills enjoy opportunity and earning power. But the others face a new and stark problem—exclusion on a permanent basis both as producers and consumers, from economic life.[15]

Thus the urban Negro not only is confronted with the traditional social problems associated with being a Negro

[13] Taeuber and Taeuber, op. cit.
[14] Taeuber and Taeuber, "The Negro as an Immigrant Group," *American Journal of Sociology*, 69, No. 4 (January 1964), 374-382.
[15] Cited by Sidney Peck and David M. Cohen, "The Social Context of De Facto School Segregation," *Western Reserve Law Review*, 16, No. 3 (May 1965), 599.

in a white-dominated America, but also, being the newest addition to the labor force, is the first to face the impact of joblessness in an automated economy. Large numbers of lower-class urban Negroes are finding themselves without economic function and increasingly removed from the good life enjoyed by other Americans. The impact of this situation has been described by Wilhelm and Powell, who write:

> The tremendous historical change for the Negro is taking place in these terms; he is not needed. He is not so much unwanted as unnecessary; not so much abused as ignored. The dominant whites no longer need to exploit him. If he disappears tomorrow he would hardly be missed. As automation proceeds it is easier and easier to disregard him . . . thus he moves to the automated urbanity of "nobodiness."[16]

Yet the industrial urban society offers great hope for the Negro in his struggle for full equality. It is a society that rewards people increasingly on the basis of needed skills rather than on the basis of race or sex. Indeed, the legal barriers to discrimination are the memorable achievements of the 1960s. With these barriers falling away, Negroes with advanced skills have been able to move into the larger society. Of course, lags persist. Middle-class Negroes are faced with persistent patterns of social discrimination and residential segregation. Their children attend the *de facto* segregated schools, which do not appear to be preparing them for social mobility. They resort to many of the same tactics all middle-class parents use to exercise some control over their children's experiences. Thus they join Parent-Teachers' Associations or send their youngsters to private schools. They have, in desperation, supported some school boycotts.

It is for the lower-class Negro, however, that the conse-

[16] Sidney M. Wilhelm and Elwin H. Powell, "Who Needs the Negro?" *Trans-Action*, 1, Issue 6 (September/October 1964), 3-6.

quences of an ineffective school system are tragic, for without successful achievement in the school the Negro youngster early in his life is denied access to economic productivity and a share in the American dream. American educational institutions play a crucial role in determining whether or not this nation will remain free from social class or race barriers to individual achievement and vertical mobility. Indeed, school failure or success has become critical in determining the life chances of the young.

> *De facto* school segregation is the social expression of this crucial role which urban schools play in "tracking" the young into favored and unfavored slots in the *organized society*. Slum children of color who do not make the grade not only drop out of school, but, are in effect dropped out of the *organized system*, since for them there is nowhere to go but down and out.[17]

For the Negro youth, the seriousness of the problem is compounded by his membership in still another American minority group, the young. As our industrial society has grown in wealth, we have extended the years during which we do not need the productive labor of young people. We keep millions of unproductive youngsters in our schools for longer and longer periods of time, for it has become necessary to keep youngsters separated from a society that has no useful place for them except as consumers. This major youth problem of our times has been described as "a steady relative breakdown in this absorption of the young non-college graduate into the work force."[18] The increased educational levels required for employment are only in part a reflection of the demand for advanced skills in an automated economy. There is increasing evidence that competition for available employment, rather than the demands of

[17] Peck and Cohen, *op. cit.*
[18] Robert A. Dentler, "Dropouts, Automation, and the Cities," *Teachers College Record*, 65, No. 6 (March 1964), 480.

technology itself, has enabled employers to raise educational requirements for jobholders.[19] The employment picture for young people with lower levels of education is bleak. For a Negro youth, the handicap of being nonwhite places him at an even greater disadvantage.[20] Educational achievement at ever higher levels has become essential for success in the race for available employment that provides the key to socioeconomic advance.

For those who are financially able and successful academically, a prolonged tenure in school is satisfactory, and the years of economic production can be postponed. But for the child who is unsuccessful and the child who is not receiving rigorous training to equip him with advanced skills for constructive living in a cybernetics-oriented society, the school can be a reservoir of hopelessness and despair to be treated with apathy, indifference, defiance, negativism, and open resistance.

Recognizing the significance of education for equipping the Negroes for full participation in society once the legal barriers to full equality have been removed, Negro civil-rights leaders, who themselves have become active participants in our society by means of education, are deeply concerned that the Negro urban poor become committed to the importance and value of formal education. They have recognized that without this commitment, the opportunity for mobility in our society is extremely limited.

The urban poor, whether white or Negro, have not been, as a group, so fully committed to the formal educational process as other, more affluent groups. Part of this stems from the fact that many of the urban poor are of relatively recent rural origin. The unskilled farm work that occupied this population did not require the formal educational levels

[19] Abram J. Jaffe and Walter Adams, "Educational Attainment and Modern Technology," *The Statistical News*, Vol. 16, No. 4 (December 1964).
[20] Dentler, *op. cit.*

that industrial technology did. Financial barriers to schooling have also characterized this group. Racial barriers to schooling and jobs served to channel the poor Negro's drive for success into such areas as sports and entertainment. Another factor is the social distance that exists between lower-class people and the schools.

Some of the ways in which Negro leaders seek to encourage concern for schooling are new and strange to educators. Boycotts, sit-ins, and street demonstrations, frequently led by members of the ministry, and which include the participation of children, seem an unorthodox way to improve the schools and develop concern for education. It is important to recognize, however, that some parents, as their concern increased, came to view the school as deliberately withholding educational opportunities from their children through poor teachers, poor facilities, and segregation. Such a view lends itself to militant action, action that is directed against the very educators who think they are doing a heroic job in the face of dreadful obstacles. It should be emphasized that these parents' anger at the schools—undignified socially and even legally often unacceptable—actually represents a tremendous growth in concern for better schooling for their children and an acute awareness that the schooling received by a child will affect his status in the economic and social structure.

3. THE "600" SCHOOLS

FOR SOME in the civil-rights movement, the most vivid symbol of the more widespread problems faced by lower-status youth has been the existence of special schools set aside to deal with the youngsters who can no longer get along in regular schools. Special provision for "problem" pupils are made in almost all urban school systems in the nation. Where a distinct school division is not organized to deal with the situation or where numbers of such children are so large that the division is unable to absorb all cases, special classes are organized. Sometimes these are known as "adjustment" classes or "opportunity" classes. These special schools and classes are viewed as custodial, a well as authoritarian, by those who oppose them, and as representing the last exit from the organized system—the final closing of the door to entrance into the larger society. That this should be the case often strikes educators as odd.

Operation Shutdown began with an effort to close one of

these special schools—called "600" schools—in New York
City. This move became one of the most controversial aspects of the shutdown, both within the protest movement
and without. It aroused much heated reaction and received
great publicity in the press. In fact, Operation Shutdown is
more comomnly known as the " '600' School Boycott" than
as "Operation Shutdown," the name given by its sponsors.

In order to understand the "600" school issue more fully
we need to look at these schools in some detail.

The "600" schools, so numbered to distinguish them from
other schools, were established by the Board of Education
of New York City in May 1946. They were designed for "the
education of children so severely emotionally disturbed or
socially maladjusted as to make continuance in a regular
school hazardous to their own safety and welfare and to the
safety and welfare of the other pupils. These children were
characterized as defiant, disruptive, disrespectful and hostile to all authority."[1]

Hopefully, these schools were meant to provide a nonpunitive, therapeutic, rehabilitative environment for those
sent to them. By 1965, there were some 5,000 boys and
girls, aged five to twenty-one, attending forty-four "600"
schools in New York City. Two thousand of these attended
fifteen day "600" schools. Most of the remainder attended
residential schools in institutions maintained by religious
faiths and by such New York City departments as Hospitals,
Welfare, and Correction. Others attended treatment centers
for children with special problems; remand centers—temporary shelters for children who have been assigned to
them by the courts; and hospital schools for preadolescent
children who have been admitted to psychiatric hospitals
for observation and diagnostic evaluation.

It is to be expected that a public-school population of more

[1] "600" Schools Yesterday, Today and Tomorrow, Committee Study, June
1964–February 1965 (New York: The Board of Education, 1965), p. 1.

than a million would inevitably have its share of psychotic or deeply disturbed youngsters in need of public care. The major share of criticism against the "600" schools, levied by Reverend Galamison and other critics who supported him, however, argues that an undue number of Negro and Puerto Rican children attend these schools and that their assignment is due mainly to prejudice, which encourages inappropriate screening procedures. In addition, the "600" schools have been accused of having no licensed Negro principals, untrained teachers, poor curriculums, inadequate guidance; of using corporal punishment and frisking; of concentrating large numbers of "problem" children under one roof; and of being housed in old buildings. In short, they are seen by militant civil rightists as receiving minority-group children who have been unfairly shunted out of their regular school experience, necessary for positive life chances. In these "600" schools, the custodial role becomes prominent.

That the "600" school program was falling far short of fulfilling its stated functions of rehabilitation and therapy was well known long before the boycott. In June 1964, Dr. Calvin Gross appointed Dr. John B. King to head a committee to study these schools between June 1964 and February 1965.[2] One of the things that made some members of the Board of Education so bitter toward Reverend Galamison was that they felt he knew that a study with recommendations was being made. They believed he should have waited for the report before calling the shutdown.

Some civil-rights leaders were wary of the "600" school

[2] Earlier critical studies of these schools include Robert M. MacIver, *The 600 Day Schools*, Interim Report No. III, April, 1957; MacIver, *Students and Their Progress in 600 Day Schools*, Interim Report No. VI, December, 1957; MacIver, *Three Residential Treatment Centers*, Interim Report No. IX, March, 1958; Judge John Warren Hill, *Official Evaluation*, 1956; and The "600" Schools Supervision Association, *The Improvement of the "600" Day Schools*, 1964.

issue. James Farmer, even when he agreed to support the shutdown, did not agree to include the "600" schools. Others in the movement considered Galamison had made a tactical error on this issue, for the calling out of "emotionally disturbed youngsters" was viewed as irresponsible by many and calculated to alienate public support. Fear of the consequences and concern for what was perceived as demagogic use of "sick" children did lead many teachers to attack him bitterly. For example, "I lost all respect for him," was a frequent comment made by teachers who had supported previous boycotts. On the other hand, several "600" school teachers who were dissatisfied with conditions offered Galamison information and supported his inclusion of the schools in the shutdown.

The press played up the "600" schools boycott, giving many the impression that these schools were the prime target of the shutdown; actually, only one "600" school was involved to any significant degree. About 110 children stayed out of this school. Four other "600" schools contributed a negligible amount of boycotters. The remainder of the 2,000 to 5,000 youngsters who were absent during the shutdown came from twenty-one junior high schools and two high schools. In addition, press reports made constant references to the "schools for emotionally disturbed," neglecting to qualify that many who are placed in "600" schools are not there for psychiatrically defined emotional problems.

Shortly after the shutdown ended, the Board of Education issued its special committee's report on the "600" schools. Very clearly, the report pointed out the many problems that beset these schools, placing upon them the burdens that are overwhelming, making them targets of criticism for conditions over which they have limited control.

In answer to the charges of prejudice, the committee argued, " . . . the ethnic distribution in the '600' schools is the obvious result of the virulent dislocations in society itself and reflects the high incidence of the damage these social ills wreak upon younger as well as older members of minority groups."[3] The report candidly admitted to serious problems. The "600" schools tended to be located in old, shabby buildings, abandoned by regular schools; the courts, social agencies, and hospitals, severely overburdened and with inadequate facilities, made it necessary for the day schools to retain youngsters in urgent need of institutional care, thus interfering with the program for others. Many youngsters who should have received preventive treatment in the ordinary school environment were sent to "600" schools because of insufficient funds, interest, and personnel to help the children in the ordinary environment. Commenting on this report, the *New York Times* wrote:

> The Board of Education's special committee report on the "600" schools documents one of the serious flaws in the City's operation: handing on pressing problems from agency to agency, without effective remedial action. Eventually the accumulation of neglect explodes, and the agency which—insufficiently aided by others—has tried to do its adequate best is made to shoulder the public blame. . . .[4]

This pattern of neglect was viewed by Reverend Galamison as wreaking the greatest damage on economically disadvantaged, minority-group children. With inadequate facilities to help them achieve success in normal school surroundings, confined to "600" schools, they have received merely custodial care and been relegated to the lowest rungs of the social ladder.

The official report tells us little about the effects of the "600" school experience on the youngsters, for the reports are not based on follow-up studies in depth. As many as 3,300 children were processed by the "600" day schools,

[3] *"600" Schools Yesterday, Today and Tomorrow*, p. 57.
[4] Editorial, *New York Times*, March 11, 1965.

and at any given time the enrollment approximated 2,000, in the year 1963-1964. Of approximately 1,300 children who left the day "600" schools:

325 returned to regular schools or graduated to high schools (academic and vocational).[5]

225 were transferred to training schools.

112 received employment certificates.

165 were discharged as over 17 years.

215 transferred to other "600" schools.

125 were exempt or transferred to state hospitals or to home instruction.

90 to out-of-town addresses.

35 not found.[6]

The committee, recognizing the shortcomings of the "600" schools, recommended improvements in curriculum screening, guidance, placement, and follow-up. It suggested several administrative and staffing changes, and urged a vastly improved building program. In addition, it made recommendations for evaluation and research, as well as improved parent, community, interschool, and agency relationships. It also recommended changing the name "600" schools to "guidance schools."

Underlying the suggestions are basic concepts which are worth noting:

. . . Most of the problems which have brought boys and girls to the "600" schools started many years earlier and are related to their inability to achieve academically and to establish satisfying, wholesome interpersonal relationships. . . . The inability to achieve academically and to establish satisfying wholesome interpersonal relationships may have been the fault of the school and/or the home and community environment. It may very well be the re-

[5] We have no data on their experiences there.
[6] *"600" Schools Yesterday, Today and Tomorrow,* pp. 15-17.

sult of overwhelming pressures and serious inadequacies in all three. . . . The assignment of children to the "600" Schools must not be viewed as a punitive measure, but rather, as a remedial one, somewhat like the case of a medical doctor's assigning a child to a hospital equipped to give the kind of needed special help and treatment that he cannot get at home or in the local community. Similarly, the "600" Schools assist children who "hurt" and who have been hurt in a social and emotional rather than in a physical way. . . . Unlike other agencies the school cannot and must not ever "give-up" on any child at any age regardless of his handicaps—physical, mental, social or emotional. The special help needed by emotionally handicapped children can and must be provided for some in regular schools and some in special schools through the joint efforts of all who have an interest in and concern for their welfare.[7]

It is interesting that this committee's report recognizes that many of the boys and girls who have been assigned to "600" schools have long histories of academic and personal difficulties that may have been the fault of the school and/or the home and community environment. The recognition of the school as a possible source of problems of troubled youngsters amounts to a relatively new approach, for while increasing attention has been paid to home and community influences on learning and behavior, the role played by the school itself in engendering difficulties has been relatively neglected.[8]

Several reasons had caused Reverend Galamison to include the "600" schools in his shutdown. One of these was the belief on his part that the schools themselves were creating the problems that caused children to be sent to "600"

[7] *Ibid.,* pp. 56-57.
[8] Doxey A. Wilkerson, "Prevailing and Needed Emphases in Research on the Education of Disadvantaged Children and Youth," *Journal of Negro Education,* Summer 1964, pp. 347-348.

schools. Once in the "600" schools, the child's chances of receiving an academic education, he believed, was remote. He saw about him many youngsters who, whatever the causes of their difficulties, had not been helped by the "600" school experience. To him, the "600" schools were a vivid symbol of the hopeless future faced by lower-class Negro youths who did not acquire skills for upward mobility.

The effects of the boycott on the "600" schools and the children have been variously interpreted. Some principals of these schools viewed the effects on the children as creating restlessness and a negative attitude that took several weeks after the boycott to calm. Parents came to request that their children be transferred to regular schools. Other principals saw positive aspects in the boycott. They saw the conflict as helping to focus public attention on the need to improve and expand positively directed programs for children unable to function in the regular school environment. These principals believed they could help children turn their backs on hopelessness and start the climb upward through the system if the "600" schools were given increased financial aid and facilities and professional, therapeutically oriented programs. In an effort to remove the stigma associated with the "600" label, the Board of Education in 1966 renumbered the schools to make them indistinguishable from ordinary schools, at least in name.

Whether or not the boycott sped the issuance of the enlightened "600" school report is difficult to ascertain.

4. UNITING FOR CONFLICT

$\mathbb{A}$LTHOUGH many viewed Operation Shutdown, along with other school boycotts, as destructive to the schools and to the children who participated, appraisal of the event, in the light of sociological theory, points to many positive functional aspects.

Many sociologists have been cognizant of the fact that conflict does have positive social value.[1] Lewis Coser has written an eloquent discussion of this topic in *The Functions of Social Conflict*,[2] based on the work of Georg Simmel, the great nineteenth-century German sociologist.[3] Coser makes the point that conflict with some produces associations with others.[4] The bonds thus established with allies help to reduce social isolation and unite individuals and groups other-

[1] Among the more prominent of these in America have been Charles H. Cooley, Edward A. Ross, Albion W. Small, and Robert E. Park.

[2] Lewis Coser, *The Functions of Social Conflict* (New York: The Free Press, 1956).

[3] See Georg Simmel, *Conflict*, trans. Kurt H. Wolff (New York: The Free Press, 1955).

[4] Coser, *op. cit.*, p. 155.

wise unrelated or even antagonistic to one another. The civil-rights movement in this country has, during periods of crisis, united many different factions in the Negro and white communities. We shall see that the school shutdown did precisely this for many diverse Negro youths in New York City. Struggle with an enemy, whether real or imagined, has the purpose, or unwitting result, of maintaining unity and internal cohesion. Thus, conflict with the Board of Education rallied otherwise apathetic, angry, and even demoralized young people, together with informed, concerned youngsters, into a unified group. In the absence of conflict the youth groups have tended to fall away and go their separate, sometimes personally and socially destructive, ways.

Not all the boys and girls who participated in the boycott had had previous experience and knowledge of the organized civil-rights movement. There were some, like the sons and daughters of the members of the Harlem Parents Committee and the Parents' Workshop for Equality in Education in Brooklyn, who had been closely associated with the movement. Several of these youngsters had even been to Selma, Alabama and in the March on Washington and had participated actively in the school boycotts of the previous year.

The larger number of the children, however, had not been, prior to the boycott, identified with the civil-rights movement in an organized way at all. In the Manhattan freedom school, run for boycotting pupils by the Charter Group for a Pledge of Conscience, for example, the leaders of the school found that less than half the participants had ever heard the song, "We Shall Overcome." Although the youngsters were familiar with the names of Martin Luther King and Malcolm X, both of whom were widely discussed on radio and television and in newspaper headlines, they had never heard of James Farmer or Milton Galamison.

It is highly significant that the conflict with the Board of

Education seems to have reached many who have been most alienated from the schools, for example, the truants. The attack levied by some educators that the boycott appealed to "hysterical elements" was a reflection of the fact that the boycott leaders welcomed the support of those with the least status and prestige, including "600" school children and their parents, dropouts, and truants. The boycott leaders sought to focus the dissatisfactions of these youngsters and their parents onto demands for a more meaningful school experience. In the absence of such focused conflict, lower-class youths have at times turned to a latter-day nihilism and anarchy, as was witnessed in the highly destructive riots in Los Angeles in the summer of 1965.

Participation in the shutdown provided the youngsters studied with the opportunity to express their dissatisfaction with the school and with their minority-group status. We shall see in later chapters that they were encouraged by their adult and peer leaders to regard education as the key to improvement of their position in society.

For committed, militant members of the Citywide Committee for Integrated Education and the Harlem Parents Committee, Operation Shutdown offered the opportunity to express their urgent demands for the kind of educational system they believed would enable their youngsters to receive preparation equal to that of whites and essential for economic mobility in our twentieth-century urban society.

During the boycott, however, not only were pressures being brought on the city school system to implement new programs, but leaders also sought to enlist in the struggle children and parents previously uninvolved in organized social protest.

FREEDOM SCHOOLS

Adult leaders of school boycotts have recognized the need to provide facilities for children who are asked not to attend public school. For this reason they have organized freedom schools.[5] The freedom schools have provided the organizational context within which grievances can be expressed and attitudes toward education crystallized. They have also provided for experience in the development of organizational skills and practice in social protest.

When the Citywide Committee for Integrated Education and the Harlem Parents Committee called for a school shutdown, a number of freedom schools were established. It was primarily the boys and girls who came to the freedom schools who participated actively in the picketing of schools, the sending of delegations to various leaders, and the picketing of the Board of Education.

In addition to the classes offered at the freedom school in Manhattan, for example, the boys and girls met in the auditorium to plan picketing activities at their various schools and elsewhere. One delegation met with President Gallagher of City College and demanded that he support the Allen Plan. When President Gallagher said that he was all for integration and was concerning himself with the problem at the college level, one delegate called out: "Man, that's like building a house from the roof down. How'm I going to get into college if I can't get into high school?"

They wrote songs, leaflets, and picket signs; organized around picket captains; ran mimeograph machines; and distributed leaflets. The freedom school participants be-

[5] Many different types of activities have been carried on under the label "freedom school." Among these are training schools for civil-rights workers in the South and leadership development programs. Freedom schools have also been organized to provide citizenship-training programs in voter-registration drives. Tutorial and remedial programs for Negro school children have also been called freedom schools. Freedom schools have provided anything from custodial to formal school programs for children participating in school boycotts. See David W. Johnson, *Changes in Self and Racial Attitudes of Negro Children Derived from Participation in a Freedom School*, unpublished paper (New York: Institute of Urban Studies, Teachers College, Columbia University, 1964).

came the leaders of the shutdown, a movement that depended primarily upon support and participation by the boys and girls.

Several schools were set up in Brooklyn, including one at the Apollo Theater and several at small churches. The school at the Siloam Presbyterian Church, under Reverend Galamison, soon became the only one functioning in Brooklyn throughout the boycott. In Manhattan, the Charter Group for a Pledge of Conscience, an organization that considers itself in the abolitionist tradition, volunteered to staff a school for the Harlem Parents Committee. (See Figure, p. 117) The schools at Siloam Presbyterian Church and the school run by the Charter Group for a Pledge of Conscience were the most significant, handled the most children, and provided us with our data on the children and their experiences.

Both schools operated under emergency conditions. However, a major difference did exist between the two in that the Manhattan freedom school, although it had no permanent quarters, did have a staff that included persons who were professionally qualified to teach and administer a school. Although only two members of this staff were permanent, volunteer teachers, many of them with professorial rank in universities within the city, came several mornings or afternoons to teach. Volunteer parents and teen-agers, including junior-high, high-school, and college students, staffed the others.

The Manhattan Freedom School

The Manhattan school was started on February eighth at the Chapel of the Intercession. The assistant vicar of this Episcopal church was anxious to get the children boycotting a nearby junior high school off the streets. On the first Monday it was in operation, about sixteen girls had received permission from their parents to attend. By 9:30, some sixty youngsters who had seen leaflets advertising the school came. Of these children, according to information gathered by the director of the school, less than one-third had fathers; about one-third lived with guardians, grandmothers, or aunts; the rest lived with their mothers and stepfathers. Later some twenty youngsters arrived from three other junior high schools.

Of all the children, only very few looked really poor. Their shoes were bad, their bodies were thin, and they devoured hungrily the two or three sandwiches apiece that were provided by the school. The teachers of this school noted that the others all looked well, wore clothing in good condition, and brought or bought their lunches. There were under 500 children involved, and the greatest number that appeared at any one time was 225.

The continuity in staff was provided by Dr. Annette Rubinstein, former principal of the Robert Louis Stevenson School and an active leader of the Charter Group for a Pledge of Conscience, and her eighty-year-old mother, a former mathematics teacher. Several college students came to help, but most of the volunteer staff were university teachers.

This school attempted to provide a formal curriculum under these rather hectic circumstances, and the children were asked to volunteer for classes. (See Figure, p. 118) The youngsters showed a marked preference for college-oriented classes and those that had greater prestige. For example, French was popular, Spanish not. Many volunteered for tutorials in algebra, whereas few volunteered for arithmetic.

Recognizing the inadequacy of the space available at the Chapel of the Intercession, the Harlem Parents Committee requested permission to establish the school at the Riverside Church. The Council of the Church agreed to grant this permission, and the school moved there on February 15,

March 3, 1965

Dear Colleague,

The inclosed letter is, I think, self-explanatory. I am sure you will want to help by setting aside a few hours a week for such volunteer tutorial work under the auspices of the Harlem Parents Committee, which is responsible for "OPERATION SHUTDOWN" in Manhattan.

Will you let me know, by returning the form below, what time you can make available weekly, and which subjects you would like to handle?

We will secure the regular textbooks of the appropiate grades for your guidance. The science is "general science" of an introductory nature. If you have had any experience at all with a remedial reading program, please indicate that specifically.

Thank you for your cooperation.

Sincerely,

A.T. Rubinstein

(Annette T. Rubinstein for the Charter Group for a Pledge of Conscience which sponsored the Freedom School referred to in the inclosed letter.)

....

Available	Mornings		Afternoons	Evenings
Monday	_____		_____	_____
Tuesday	_____		_____	_____
Wednesday	_____		_____	_____
Thursday	_____		_____	_____
Friday	_____		_____	_____

	Algebra	Arithmetic	Remedial Reading	General English
Can tutor	____	____	____	____

	French	Spanish	Social Studies	Science
Can tutor	____	____	____	____

Name_____

Address_____

Telephone_____

FACSIMILE OF APPEAL FOR STAFFING FREEDOM SCHOOLS ISSUED DURING OPERATION SHUTDOWN.

A CALL TO CONSCIENCE

As citizens of the United States and residents of New York City, we have observed with anger and frustration the upsurge of racism, the accelerating separation of the races in the last year, and the callous disregard by our city officialdom of the just demands of our Negro and Puerto Rican citizens.

Racism is at the heart of the refusal of New York to come to grips with the unbearable conditions of life imposed upon a million and a half New Yorkers.

We refuse any longer to permit our city to run down the disastrous path of Birmingham, Alabama, Jackson, Mississippi, and Albany, Georgia. Our racism differs from that of Birmingham, Jackson and Albany only in the hypocrisy of our public utterances.

In the name of the "Open City," we have permitted housing segregation to grow through public and private building. We have ignored the rat-infested, neglected slums and winked at those who profit from the overcrowding and deterioration made possible by enforced segregation.

In the name of "School Integration," we have paired eight schools while continuing to build and plan for the construction of hundreds of new, segregated schools; we tolerate a dual system that favors the privileged and keeps fully half of our public school children illiterate and imprisoned in inferior ghetto schools.

We declare a "war on poverty" while permitting discrimination in employment, and less than subsistence wages, for Negro and Puerto Rican workers.

We turn our backs on the youth of our city, while nearly 40 per cent of the Negro and Puerto Rican teenagers are out of work and despair of ever finding a job. In a budget of 3.3 billion dollars, New York could not, this summer, find $112,000 to continue the jobs of 630 teenagers as promised by Mayor Wagner. And then we remain silent while the public press daily attacks the youth of the ghettoes and slums as hoodlums.

When the people of the Harlems of our city, in their anger and frustration, rise up to demand redress of their grievances, we greet them with offical indifference, public hysteria and police bullets.

By day, the white community profits through segregation; by night, the white community walks in fear of the real and imagined terrors it has evoked.

The Negro community is fighting these evils. Whoever in the white community is silent today is in fact condoning them. We call on those citizens of New York who have been silent only because they could not find a way to make their voices heard, to come together, in the spirit of the Abolitionist societies of a hundred years ago, to expose the nature of our segregated way of life and do all that may be necessary to change it.

Charter Group for a Pledge of Conscience   P.O. Box 346
                                                            Cathedral Station
                                                            New York, N.Y. 10025

FACSIMILE OF AN APPEAL FOR SUPPORT ISSUED BY THE
SPONSORS OF MANHATTAN FREEDOM SCHOOLS DURING
OPERATION SHUTDOWN.

1965. As the Rev. Eugene Laubach, executive minister of the Riverside Church explained, " . . . a number of our own teen-agers were involved in the situation, so we preferred to try to make a facility available. We felt that at least it would give them a place to go."[6]

To this school came more children from nearby schools. Four classes and an auditorium were available. Again, a formal curriculum was provided, and once more preference for traditional college-oriented courses was indicated. This concern for algebra and language was the result of the realistic appraisal of requirements for an academic High School Regents' diploma, one that would enable students to qualify for higher education. It is at this critical point, junior high school, that movement out of the academic track makes for blocking of college entrance. We shall refer later to comments by the children concerning their experiences in this freedom school and to lessons learned outside of the mathematics and French tutorials. However, it is interesting to note that these children were not interested in attending a film on Africa shown by the school, nor were they particularly interested in learning about American Indians from an anthropologist. They showed much greater interest in a talk on urban sociology offered by one university professor.

The head of the Manhattan freedom school commented that these youngsters were "the most poorly educated I have seen in my life." She was very impressed with the intelligence of the youngsters and with their verbal ability but was appalled at their lack of academic knowledge. For example, several could not subtract; yet within a short time, she said, they became quite competent under the tutelage of freedom school teachers. Many could not read numbers with decimal points. She believed that their memories were

[6] Quoted in the *New York Times*, February 23, 1965.

very good and that they had excellent vocabularies closely related to TV and radio language, but that they were not good readers.

Dr. Rubinstein was surprised by her inability to establish a pattern of order and discipline. She found the youngsters very friendly and cheerful, yet she received less cooperation than she had expected. This she attributed to the fact that they were antiestablishment, and this feeling overshadowed any short-lived alliance they had with the teachers in the freedom school.

However, the lessons learned in this and other freedom schools far transcend the grasping of reading and algebra. As we examine the experiences of the participants in a later chapter, we shall become aware of the larger lessons learned.

When the Board of Education attendance officers asked the Riverside Church to discontinue the school because it violated the state education law in "harboring children during school hours," the Church Council took the position that it could not endorse the school boycott and asked the freedom school to leave. By February twenty-third, the Manhattan freedom school had to move again, this time to St. Mary's Episcopal Church, again for a limited period of time, because of commitments for use of the church that had been made previously. Thus, the first week in March saw the close of this freedom school.

Brooklyn Freedom Schools

In Brooklyn, several small schools were set up to handle boycotting pupils. One group of youngsters persuaded the management of the Apollo Theater, a local vaudeville house, to open its doors to them for a school. Here, too, attendance officers appeared and informed the management concerning the compulsory-attendance laws. The freedom school was then evicted.

_____

. Do Not Write in This Space
.
. Date:_____
.
. Recorder:_____

I P L E D G E:

 To conduct myself

 according to the

 best rules of behavior.

****
*   *
* YOUR CHILDREN know what prejudiced   *
*   teachers are like!   *
*   *
* YOUR CHILDREN know they are not   *
*   being taught!   *
*   *
* YOUR CHILDREN know what it means   *
*   to be second class students!   *
*   *
* D O   Y O U ?   *
****

Name:_____   Age: _____

Address:_____   Phone:_____

School: _____   Grade:_____

****

I,_____, parent or guardian of the above

named child, consent to his/her attendance at the above addressed Freedom School,

open daily 8:30 a.m. to 1:30 p.m.

****

FACSIMILE OF ATTENDANCE RECORD USED IN BROOKLYN
FREEDOM SCHOOLS DURING OPERATION SHUTDOWN,
FEBRUARY—MARCH, 1965.

March 3, 1965

Dear Parent,

You probably know that a large group of well qualified Negro and white teachers helped us by running a February Freedom School for the Junior High School Students out on strike during the first month of the school shutdown.

Now these fine teachers have offered to continue their help by tutoring students in all the regular Junior High School subjects - mathematics, English, foreign languages, social studies and science - so that our children will not fall behind in their work because of the shutdown, or the general poor conditions in their Junior High Schools.

If your son or daughter would like to get free private lessons from one of these excellent teachers, please fill in the paper below and mail or bring it in to us at the Harlem Parents Committee, 514 West 126th St.

We will immediately arrange to have your child get a free private lesson twice a week with a good teacher in each subject he needs help with. These lessons will begin next week, and continue until the end of the regular school year in June.

Don't lose time. Send the form below back to us today.

Joseph Patterson, Vice-Chairman
Harlem Parents Committee

JP:ns

....

I would like to have my child get free private lessons in (check each subject) :

Algebra_____, Arithmetic_____, English_____, Reading_____, French_____,

Spanish_____, Social Studies_____, Science_____.

My child's full name is_____.

My child is in the 7th_____, 8th_____, 9th_____grade in

Junior High School #_____.

Parent's or Guardian's name_____

Adress_____

Telephone_____

FACSIMILE OF QUESTIONNAIRE DISTRIBUTED TO PARENTS AFTER
OPERATION SHUTDOWN.

Very early in the shutdown, the Siloam Presbyterian Church, the pastor of which was the Rev. Mr. Galamison, became the main freedom school for Brooklyn. Several features distinguished this school. One was the absence of trained adult teachers and supervisors. Much of the organizational work was undertaken by the Parents' Workshop for Integrated Education, a group that met in the church to consider problems of integration. Many of the youngsters attracted to the school helped take part in running it. Later we shall hear some of them describe what happened here. In addition, this particular school attracted some of the boycotting "600" school youngsters, some of whom belonged to the church or lived in the immediate neighborhood. In general, this school was less formally organized, encompassed many diverse and bickering groups of boys and girls, and was unable to provide a curriculum parallel to that offered in the public schools. Yet it would be a mistake to dismiss the activities as purely chaotic and undisciplined, for there, too, as we shall see, many lessons were learned.

The Participants Speak

5. HOW THEY JOINED THE BOYCOTT

ORIGINALLY the call for the boycott came from the adult organizations. Very early, however, the children were involved in the planning and organization necessary to carry out the action, thereby gaining experience in types of planning and organizational skills demanded in our society. The initial leaders in this regard were children already associated with the movement through their parents' involvement. They were also children who were familiar with evidence that documented the inferior achievement of children in the schools they attended. This evidence was confirmed by their own personal experiences.

GIRL:
We're 8-honor, that's an SP class and we can't even get by with fractions.[1] And most of us can't spell or nothing

[1] An SP Class refers to Special Progress classes for intellectually gifted children. The 8-19 exponent refers to the nineteenth class at the eighth grade; as the classes are organized according to reading level in this school, the highest exponent would represent the class lowest in academic achievement.

and I'd like to see some of those 8-19 class if we can't spell. And so anyway we came down to the church and we found out about the segregation in our school and we decided well there had to be something to be done and since it looked like nobody else was going to do it, we had to do it ourselves. There was four of us girls and we started out . . . we went around we had petitions signed and we talked to people and we got money and we did so many things—we just tied in everything. . . .

Another girl whose mother was involved describes her participation in the organization of the shutdown. This girl believed that the schools in white sections of the borough were superior.

GIRL:

. . . we were just comparing the difference between integration and segregation. And the white, they're all . . . the predominantly white schools out in Flatbush and the Negro schools out in Bedford-Stuyvesant. So we was comparing them and we said that something needs to be done about them. And so then I told them about Reverend Galamison was supposed to be having another boycott, a shutdown. Then we decided to get a committee up of our own, you know, for our school—you know, helping to shut down our school and we call ourselves "The Fighters of————." And then we held a meeting one Monday and that, you know, the kids' ideas on what they wanted to do and how they wanted to go about, you know, shutting down the school.

INTERVIEWER:

Uh huh. And that's how the committee started?

GIRL:

Yes. And then we typed up petitions, we went out and got petitions signed and everything and we have over 400 members.

INTERVIEWER:

What did the petition say?

GIRL:

>Oh, it just said, "We, the undersigned, students of
———, protest segregated education," and so on and
so forth and, you know, we had the students sign their
name, address, and telephone numbers. And then we
send out mailings, you know, for our meeting and we,
you know, get on the phone sometimes . . . a lot of the
kids don't have telephones so we send out letters.

Although some of the boys and girls who participated in
the boycott were the sons and daughters of thc adults who
supported the organizations involved, the shutdown also
attracted many who had not previously been related to active roles in these types of organizations. For example, when
the freedom school run by the Charter Group for a Pledge of
Conscience opened its doors at the Chapel of Intercession,
twelve to sixteen girls who had parental permission attended, but sixty who had received leaflets in the morning
from pickets in front of the school also showed up. As word
got around that there were facilities at the school, including gymnasium in the afternoon, the school was swamped
with youngsters, many of whom were regularly truant. That
the boycott attracted many who had had no previous civil-
rights organization involvement is quite clear. We have already seen how some were attracted to the freedom schools
by leaflets. Some went along with friends. Others, already
out of school either as truants or dropouts, were attracted
by the "action," by something going on that appeared interesting.

BOY:

>I had just come back from the employment office and
I was coming down this way—I was going up to Fulton
Street to JOIN,[2] see if I could get something down there

[2] JOIN, "Job Orientation in Neighborhoods," an agency of the Mayor's
office and one of New York City's antipoverty programs.

JOIN
THE STRUGGLE FOR
INTEGRATED SCHOOLS
Participate with your fellow
students and DEMAND the
immediate implementation of
the Allen Plan

Monday, March 8th
4:00 PM
to the steps of the
Board of Ed.

Picket against N.Y.C.
segregated school system

THE ONLY EDUCATION IS
QUALITY INTEGRATED
EDUCATION.

sponsored by:
Student Committee for
Integrated Education

FACSIMILE OF LEAFLET DISTRIBUTED DURING OPERATION
SHUTDOWN, FEBRUARY—MARCH, 1965.

—and they was telling me about this Freedom School. They said, "Jim, why don't you go————?" . . . some girl told me—a girl I knew, she told me, "Well, Jimmy, go to the church, there's something happening there." I said, "Yeah." I goes on in here and I see a lot of colored children down here and as I go upstairs, you know, it look like I see more children, you know. And I went up to the concert hall and I see all them kids in there and I just came down here and all of a sudden I found myself a member of the Citywide Committee for Integrated Schools.

At least one loyal participant, a school dropout, was inadvertently recruited by the police.

BOY:
See I was . . . I was going downtown one day to see this lawyer. And I seen all these people downtown, you know. They wasn't boycotting the Board of Education building, it was the Board of Health building. So I was stopped to look and I seen my friend————. I seen him . . . he was getting arrested so I started laughing. I said: "Look. There go————." And we all started laughing. The police came over and picked us up. I said, "What did we do?" He said, "You all are disorderly." So they took us down . . .
INTERVIEWER:
Even though you weren't even part of the boycott they took you?
BOY:
Yeah, they took us down to the precinct and we stayed there for about eight hours and then they took us over in New York to court. And we stayed . . . first we stayed in the jail for about three days before we went to court. And our bail was $2,500.00.[3]

[3] The sum actually represents a composite figure of bail for a number of youngsters.

INTERVIEWER:

$2,500! Who put up the bail for you?

BOY:

The church. And that's when I first learned about the church when they brought us out. Because I said, "I know my mother ain't bailed me out for that much money!" So when I came out of jail . . . you know, that was . . . we had stayed in there three days. They brought us back to Brooklyn and we stayed at Atlantic Avenue for three days before they brought us out. And they told us what it was all about. So they asked us to come down to the church. So I started coming down to the church every day. So here I am down here now.

INTERVIEWER:

Was there any time when you were afraid when you were part of the boycott, or any time you were sorry you were part of it or that you were afraid?

BOY:

No.

INTERVIEWER:

Would you march again if they had another one?

BOY:

Yes. Nothing like the first . . . when I got arrested, you know, I wasn't even with them and that was the only time I say, "All those stupid people out in the street and I go and get arrested for them."

We have said that, for many of the children participating in the shutdown, there had been at first little concern or understanding for the social-protest aspects of their absence from school. They were attracted to the freedom schools by curiosity, by their peer connections, and by the adult leaders who asked them to come and help. No one intimately connected with the situation doubts that many of the youngsters were happy to have a chance to stay out of school—something many of them had been doing all along anyway as truants, even without the organized shut-down—but they seemed pleased to have something to do with their time they felt was worthwhile, and they were ready to express their grievances concerning their schooling.

6. THE PURPOSE OF THE BOYCOTT

THE BOYS AND GIRLS attracted to the various freedom schools were asked by their leaders, both adults and peers, to consider why they were staying out of school. Thus there arose the opportunity for crystallizing the reasons for their discontent. As the youngsters verbalized their discontent, they began to see some purpose in the boycott.

One of the things that is impressive is the fact that the various participants had various reasons for staying out. Reasons also varied from school to school, for not every school presented the same kind of problem.

At the freedom school run by the Charter Group for a Pledge of Conscience, in Manhattan, a group discussion was held with junior-high youngsters. They were asked to pretend that they were in a radio station, responding to an interviewer who asked, "Why are you in the shutdown?" Among the answers given were that they wanted better teachers—one group of youngsters complained that its mathematics class had had nine teachers that year; it complained that their teachers couldn't handle the class; some complained that they had some teachers who beat them. Other complaints included comments about "crummy" buildings, no swimming, and no books. Some of the children referred to teachers who called them "nigger." One teacher was said to call them "kinky head."[1] The one teacher some of the youngsters spoke of with respect was a member of CORE and a strict disciplinarian who could control his class well.

Those youngsters who had been part of the civil-rights organization felt very strongly that integrated education was essential to enable the Negro child to compete with the white child for employment on an equal basis. Thus they avidly supported the shutdown, for they felt it necessary to make the Board of Education take a more active role in making for improved racial balance in the schools.

In the course of organizing the boycott they urged that people take their education very seriously, the leaders specifically acquainting others with the notion that education was so important that they should protest conditions in the schools they attended. Although apparently walking out on schooling by participation in the boycott, many of these youngsters were in effect actually identifying very strongly with the belief that, through education and improved schooling, they would be given the tools enabling them to move into a position of fuller equality in American society. They were acutely conscious of whites' being in a superior status to

[1] These complaints are strikingly similar to the ones noted by Florence Howe, who, in a report on children in Freedom Schools in Mississippi, writes, "They resented their hand-me-down textbooks, they suspected the inadequacy of their teachers, and they complained particularly bitterly about the repressive atmosphere." Florence Howe, "Mississippi's Freedom Schools: The Politics of Education," *Harvard Educational Review*, 35, No. 2 (Spring 1965), 154.

themselves. They felt very strongly that it was through inferior education that their lower-class position was maintained.[2] This could be seen in their remarks on a number of subjects.

GIRL:
. . . we told those kids what was happening in our school. We told them that if they didn't get out and do something now, probably they would be nowhere and they would get no job or anything. Because, we said, "How can you get a job without an education or how can you get anything without an education?" If you don't have an education, you have nothing. And that they would like to visit some of the white . . . where the white students go to school—they would be amazed because those kids really, they're all the way up, you know.

And we told them how . . . some of the people explained to most of the kids how some of their sons and daughters dropped out of school because they couldn't compete with the other kids because people were passing by them, the white kids and everything, and they dropped out of school.

And we went around, we told people and we had a lot of great responses. We started out with four of us and we had four hundred members in about three or four weeks. It was really great. People listened, things like, kids listen to kids, like if you're a teen-ager you can talk to another teen-ager because you understand them, I think. It was real great.

Although they did not discuss the Allen Report in detail, the participants felt that the Board of Education had done little to fulfill the promise of action to integrate the schools,

[2] It is interesting to note that in this respect the arguments for racial integration in schooling parallel the arguments for coeducation.

a move they regarded as essential to improved education. They also felt that the Board was not listening to them:

GIRL:
Well, we feel like this, the other kids and I feel . . . we had to have a conference with the Board of Education, we had to sit down and talk with them . . .

INTERVIEWER:
Did you actually sit down and talk with them? I mean, with the Board of Education?

GIRL:
. . . no, adults went. And Reverend Galamison has gone, we wrote them letters, sent in petitions and everything. They just overlooked it like, packed them there at the bottom of the file. So we said if we can't do it quietly without demonstrations, we would have to demonstrate. So we demonstrated.

With one exception, the youngsters we interviewed felt that integration was an essential ingredient to better schooling, and they supported the boycott's attack on *de facto* segregated schools. The belief that teachers would teach better if the classes contained white children was expressed frequently. One young man, when asked what he believed to have been the purpose of the boycott, said:

BOY:
. . . to have a equal amount of white and Negroes and Puerto Ricans going to the same schools so they can all get the same education. Because they believe if Negroes and whites go to the same schools, then if the teacher don't want to teach Negroes nothing then the white people won't learn nothing; and if the teacher wants to teach the white children, so then they have to teach the Negro children too because they all going to the same school. They want everybody to get the same equal education.

INTERVIEWER:
How do you feel about it? Do you feel this?

BOY:

Yeah! It's a good idea. Because they right. The teachers, they don't care about teaching no Negro children
because, like my teacher, he say: "I don't care if you
don't learn. I'm getting paid for it anyway"—in an all-
colored high school. Like when I was in———, a
teacher never said that because there are white children
in my class. They all taught; everybody learned the
same thing. But at———, the things I learned at
———, ———ain't even got these things yet. They're
still on the junior high school and it's a high school.
And they still teaching you them junior-high-school
subjects.

Over and over the boys and girls expressed the belief that
the boycott was for integrated schooling, which they viewed
as essential as a prerequisite for training equal to that given
white children.

BOY:

. . . like you go to an all-white school, you see them
sitting up there with brand-new books and you go to a
de facto segregated high school and see them sitting
up there with raggedy books, taped up covers and everything. . . . Everybody gets tired of this. Everybody can't
stand raggedy things. And another reason is so . . . so
colored people, so colored people can have the same
jobs the white person has but this particular boycott
that they had right here, that was for schools. They
wanted . . . to put more white children inside colored
schools so that the colored kids will have the same
equal rights that the white people have.

INTERVIEWER:

Do you think if they put whites in schools with Negroes
or Negroes in schools with whites that the education
would be better or improved? How do you feel?

BOY:

Yeah, it would be improved.

INTERVIEWER:
Why?
BOY:
Because you figure like this here—they don't want the white children to come out dumb like the colored children. They know that if the colored children don't get treated right he's not going to act right. So that's the way I see it.

Among other reasons for joining the boycott was the objection to overcrowding in schools. At least one boy stated a basic pedagogical quarrel he had with heterogeneous ability groupings in classes. Although he too felt that the purpose of the boycott was to enable him to get a better education, he held strong opinions on how school could help him.

INTERVIEWER:
What do you think was the real purpose of the boycott?
BOY:
Well, you need better schools, better schooling, and the teachers, they . . . the teacher doesn't teach the kids and they want to integrate the schools.
INTERVIEWER:
When you say teachers don't teach the kids, what do you mean?
BOY:
Well, they see the kids . . . instead of placing them in a class together, the kids that are slower group—they should place them in one class and the ones in another class that's faster in learning. And then teach them in a slower class—build up their reading, mathematics and so forth, build it up. Then you could place them back over here.
INTERVIEWER:
But instead, what do they do?
BOY:
You just go along with that group and you just gets

behind. And then that's why a lot of people drop out of school. They feel that they'll never be able to learn.

We have seen that these youngsters are acutely conscious of whites' enjoying a superior status to themselves. They feel very strongly that it is deliberately, through inferior education, that their lower-class position is maintained. They believe that only militant action will force change to occur. One young girl expressed this feeling clearly.

GIRL:

But, when you're out there and you want something . . . you want your freedom . . . we don't want our freedom on an installment plan and we don't want our education the same way either. And that's the way I feel—and I feel this way—if you want something, the only way to get it is to go out there and fight for it. And if you fight for it, then you have it because people have to give—these white people have to lay off some. . . . They don't give us nothing if we don't ask for it. . . . I'm tired that white people can tell me—you can't get this —so I don't get it. They tell me you have to do without and so I do without. They say you go here, I go here. But from now on, when I want something, I'm going to get it if I have to go out there on a picket line by myself. I'll do it myself because I want my freedom and I don't want it on an installment plan. So I'm going to fight for it.

And my mother backed me all the way and I'm glad. You know, because it was really great. I thought my mother . . . her school days are over and I thought maybe she'd say, "Well no, you belong in school where you can get educated." But she backed me all the way. She was just great. As a matter of fact, she got out there on that picket line so much . . . all our mothers were just out there. It was just great, I'm telling you.

I really thought that maybe I would grow up . . . I want to be a news reporter so I said, well, my education,

I have to take it in my own hands and go out in that street and get it. So, that's exactly what I'm going to do. If Reverend Galamison calls another boycott, I'm going out there again. I'm on probation from the courts and the truant officers but, if there's another boycott, I'm going out there again. I do not care. I don't want my freedom or my education on the installment plan and I'm not going to take it that way because I'm just tired of people telling me to take it this way and I take it that way. You just get tired of those things sometimes.

Because, you know, as a kid, like my sister and everything, we all grew up in this neighborhood, we grew up in the slums in Harlem, it's really disgusting. I mean, you sit around and like you live across the street from a candy store and in back of the store where the white people live, and they used to come out and buy ice cream and all those little Negro kids would be running up and down the streets and we were real hot and everything, and those white kids would look so nice and cool in their little sun suits and everything—and they would come out with ice cream. And just to see the ice cream, it would make your mouth water but we was just so proud that we wouldn't ask them for nothing. And that's just the way we grew up. We just grew up wanting. It's like a neighborhood where when you have something that wasn't yours and that's a neighborhood where you never could get nothing. So my mother decided she was going to move into a better place and it seem like prejudice is practiced everywhere. I mean, I don't blame white people these days that don't like us Negroes or nothing like that. I think it's their parents that taught them prejudice. But, after all, they don't have to practice it. And that's exactly the way I feel. . . .

7. PUPIL GRIEVANCES

TO SOME EDUCATORS it appears paradoxical that the child who wants an education does not attend school. Why doesn't such a child avail himself of the facilities in existence? To the children we interviewed, however, the schools as they function now are viewed as deleterious. They want an education, but they feel the schools are not functioning to provide it.

THE ABSENCE OF POWER

Before turning to an examination of what the youngsters view as obstacles to a good education, it is necessary to point to the limitations pupils have in expressing their grievances. Children ordinarily have practically no effective way of making their grievances known, for they have little power within the school structure. This is true of students generally in America. Recent outbreaks of student protest, extending from the Berkeley Campus of the University of California to Yale have called attention to this problem.[1]

Younger school children are particularly vulnerable to this powerlessness. Sometimes their complaints are squelched by parents who accept the authority of the school fully and uncritically. At least, there is fear on the part of many that to hear out a child's complaints about a teacher or school is to encourage a poor attitude, rationalization for individual weakness, and an inability to "take it." In addition, there is the real concern on the part of some parents for keeping their children out of trouble for fear of possible reprisals.

Within the school itself, there is little structural provision for the airing of grievances. Schools do not encourage complaints, and more often than not administration is expected to back up the teacher, rather than the child or parent. Teachers speak approvingly of those principals who stand behind them and disparage those who take the side of the parent or child. To admit to incompetency, an error in grading, an unfairly difficult or poor examination, a discriminatory class placement, a poor homework assignment, or even a question of taste in handling discussion, is difficult, because the school personnel, not parents or children, are seen as setting the rules. These are, however, the kinds of matters that sophisticated, middle-class parents can take up with the school personnel, either the teacher himself or the administration. Thus, the middle-class child has adult advocates available to him.

Student organizations appear to provide a mechanism for expression of student views. But here again, the rules are set by the institution, and, where the grievances are defined as inappropriate from the standpoint of the school, the student cannot be heard.

Occasionally, a sympathetic teacher will provide an ear

[1] See Calvin Trillin, "Letter from Berkeley," *New Yorker*, March 13, 1965, pp. 52-107, for an enlightening discussion of the Berkeley protest.

for a disgruntled child. But even here, if the teacher is to maintain comfortable relations with the staff, he must be very discreet, even when aware of the justification of the child's complaints, and he frequently sees his role as helping the child to adjust, rather than as changing the situation. Should he assume the role of agitator for reform, he himself faces difficulties. This holds true for the guidance counselor as well. In this role, the individual is expected to listen to the children. However, he has very limited power to initiate change and once more often merely facilitates individual adjustment to conditions that remain unsatisfactory. Thus the disaffected child must accommodate to the institution, which continues to provide unsatisfactory and unpromising learning situations.[2]

Although these conditions apply to all children, the middle-class child is in the more advantageous position of having resources available to him to assist in the hazardous journey from home through school to participation in the larger society. Perhaps the most significant thing he has in his favor is the coincidence of goals set by society, the school, his parents, and himself—goals that are within the realm of possibility and for which he is prepared by compensatory and supportive mechanisms set up by himself, his family, the school, and his peers. These goals are directed toward places somewhere along the higher-status ranks in the eco-

[2] Matters of school organization, including the pedagogically questionable organization by age and segmented forty- or fifty-minute periods, matters of curriculum, and questions of attitude and climate for learning provided by staff, severely circumscribe the effectiveness of the counselor. That his energies might be better directed toward improving the school rather than changing the child has been suggested by William C. Kvaraceus who writes, ". . . personnel workers can best serve their present and future clients by addressing themselves more and more to the improvement of the curriculum of the school." William C. Kvaraceus, "Negro Youth and Social Adaptation: The Role of the School as an Agent of Change," in Kvaraceus, et al., *Negro Self-Concept: Implications for School and Citizenship* (New York: McGraw-Hill Book Co., Inc., 1965), p. 119.

nomic and social life of American society. Competition for relative places along these higher strata has become a major concern for middle-class youths.

The lower-class child has, as well, several mechanisms operating, but operating to fulfill the prophecy of low achievement and failure. Not only does he often face inferior teaching, lowered expectations, and poorer facilities, but he rarely is in a situation in which compensations in the form of tutoring by persons knowledgeable in the ways of the system, parental handling of grievances, and support from peers in his struggle operate to enable him to overcome these handicaps.[3] More significantly, there exists the overriding expectation by society that he is destined to persist in his lower-class status, that his "lower-class culture" is something he wishes to retain and will not give up, and that the chances for success are severely limited. Coming from homes where there are few of the acceptable techniques for helping the child to overcome the hazards of moving through school, surrounded by peers who themselves do not have the resources to overcome, and faced with a multitude of his fellows who have not overcome, it is only with the greatest of personal courage and strength that he does not fall victim to self-defeat but rather shouts. "We *shall* overcome!"

Not all children placidly accept the roles established for them by the school. Many suffer discomfort and acute distress from situations they view as denigrating their positions to a continuation of lower-class, subordinate positions. Thus it is in the school with predominantly lower-class Negro and white populations that we find the highest incidence of rejection of the school evinced by the children in the form of truancy, dropping out, incorrigible behavior, apathy, and inattentiveness. The alienation of these children is a major concern for American education.

---

[3] After-school homework centers have recently been established by various groups. It is too soon to know the effects of these.

Over and over again, the literature on the lower-class Negro treats these symptoms as functions of the "lower-class subculture."[4] Some authors see this subculture as having a tradition and history of its own that ensures its continuance over the centuries. One writer has even termed this the "Dregs" culture, attributing it to the leaving behind of the dregs by the more competent residents of the slum who move out of the ghetto and up the socioeconomic ladder.[5]

From the point of view of the children interviewed, however, the schools were seen as the source of their difficulty. They expressed real grievances against the schools, which they viewed as causing many of their problems.

PUPIL CRITICISMS

There are two basic areas of criticism that the boys and girls level against the schools. One has to do with pedagogy itself. Many of the teachers are viewed as incompetent or as withholding education from Negro children. The other has to do with deliberate efforts to downgrade and humiliate. Teachers who can't teach and teachers who engage in invasion of privacy and insult to personal dignity are cited over and over again. These criticisms were levied against teachers regardless of whether the teacher was white or Negro. It is the behavior of the teacher rather than his race that appears to be crucial in the view of the child.

Almost without exception, the school was, for the children, personified by the teacher. The teacher, of course, maintains the greatest amount of actual contact with the children in the school. Principals were rarely mentioned. To the

---

[4] See Walter Miller, "Lower Class Culture as a Generating Milieu of Gang Delinquency," *Journal of Social Issues,* Vol. 14, No. 3 (1958); and Miller, "Implications of Lower Class Culture for Social Work," *Social Service Review,* Vol. 33, No. 3 (September 1959).

[5] John A. Bartky, *Social Issues in Public Education* (Boston: Houghton Mifflin Co., 1963), pp. 135-138.

pupil, the principal is a remote figure. Occasionally, reference was made to a particularly authoritarian assistant-to-principal. The dean, who represents the disciplinary figure of the school, is also known and discussed. It is the individual teacher, however, who figures most prominently in the child's daily school experience.

In our interviews we found that the boys and girls were extremely critical of many of their teachers and that for them ineffective teaching was almost invariably viewed as a denial of education because of race. That more than race is involved, however, becomes apparent from their comments about Negro teachers. Although white teachers are viewed with suspicion, Negro teachers are viewed critically also. Although teachers are sometimes seen as discriminating solely on the basis of race, the comments of several pupils reveal social-class discrimination:

GIRL:
> Well, you know, the teachers are prejudiced. Now, how would you like a Negro teacher to tell you . . . you're trying to tell her something and she tells you, "You Negroes," . . . really, she calls us niggers . . . "You niggers, you don't have no right on the street, you're not going to get . . . those white people owned you and you let yourself be enslaved and that's what you deserved." . . . and the white teacher he calls us niggers and he throws chairs at us and chases us around the room. That's not a school. That's more like a reform school, and one thing you have to do . . . The teachers put more emphasis on behavior than they do on teaching and that way you don't learn nothing. . . . I mean, a teacher going to stand up in front of the classroom a whole period while you could learn something useful for you in your future life and he's going to sit up there and tell funny stories or tell you about one of his experiences—it doesn't make no sense. That isn't teaching so as the kids can learn.

A common complaint expressed by many of the youngsters who participated in the freedom schools was that they
simply were not being taught well in public school. For example, at the Riverside Church, a frequent comment made
was: "At school they just put things on the board, they
don't explain. You explain better."

The same complaint concerning teachers who don't teach
was made over and over again. Attacks on personal dignity
made by the ineffective teacher were invariably noted. A girl
stated succinctly concerning her French teacher:

GIRL:
> I don't like my French teacher at all. I like French but
> I don't like the teacher because she figures because she
> knows French that we should know it too. And if, if you
> make a little mistake she's quick to call you stupid and
> especially me. We don't get along together at all and
> she's always calling me stupid. And so I don't like her.

One of the difficulties faced by potential dropouts was that
they had few resources outside the school to aid and support
them in academic work. Those who were unable, by themselves, to maintain satisfactory performance in school work
faced added problems when teachers did not understand
their special needs. When the teacher respected the child's
problem there was deep appreciation by her pupil. One boy
stated:

BOY:
> Well, my history teacher, she now . . . she's colored. She
> was colored. . . . Say . . . she had given you a homework
> assignment and you didn't do it and you come in the
> next day, she asks you how come you didn't do your
> homework and you tell her, she'll sit down and talk it
> over with you. But not the other teachers. Like my math
> teacher. He says, "How come you didn't do your home-
> work?" I said, "Well, I didn't understand it." He would
> say, "Well," he say, "I'll give you double that much

homework." But Miss————, she wouldn't do that, you know, she would say, "All right, I'm going to let you make it up—I'm going to let you try." She'd explain it to you. She was all right. She was one of the nicer ones of the teachers.

Another boy made the same point:

BOY:
Well like, I had some homework which I didn't understand too clearly, so after class I asked her and she told me. She usually tells me, you know. If I'm still behind and need help, she always helps. She was a white teacher. She's very nice. She helped everybody. She was very patient. And some teachers I dislike because when you go up there, "Well, ask one of your friends." And when I ask one of my friends, they don't know nothing. They can't tell me.

When the teacher attempts to exert and reinforce his authority over a youngster who has a deep resentment of his subordinate position, violence sometimes ensues. The following incident illustrates the keen sensitivity felt by one boy toward a white teacher who he felt did not treat him in such a way as to indicate respect for his dignity as a person:

BOY:
Like I've went to school two times and I had my hat on. The teacher tells me, "Take your hat off." I don't want to take it off. He tells me to take it off, I say, "Okay." Some teachers . . . they believe in a student asking them things very nicely, please, or may I, thank you. . . . Now, do unto others . . . I go by that. I definitely do, do unto others as you would have others do unto you. Now, if you was to ask a teacher a question nicely—being nice to them, you'd expect the same from them, respect.

A lot of teachers that teaches in schools do not give students the proper respect. That's why when a parent go to school she hears students in the hallway cursing

and saying things they're not supposed to be saying.
Now, for instance . . . I know, myself, I give students,
I give teachers respect. Like a woman teacher. I talk to
a woman teacher, yes ma'am, no ma'am, ma'am—a male
teacher, yes sir, no sir. I tell them that and I tell them
thank you, you welcome, and may I, and please, you
know, I believe that's . . . that's the high word in vocabulary to me. Please and thank you. They are important.

Some people don't know how to use it like, for instance, I be sitting in school and I have my hat on. The
teacher say, "Take your hat off." He don't ask me, he tell
me in a nasty tone of voice, "Take your hat off." I take
my hat off and I ask the teacher, "Why can't you say
please, like if I was asking you something I'd say please?"
Now, some teachers will do that, some of them would
say, "———, please take your hat off." "Yes sir," I take
my hat off. Some teachers walk up to you, "Get that hat
off." What kind of way is that to talk to a student? If a
student walk up to a teacher and say, "Get out of my
way, fella," the teacher'd look around at him and he may
knock his head off.

Now, I admit, a teacher has hit me before, but a
teacher never got away with it. When a teacher hit
me before, he said, "———, get that hat off." I told him,
"You say please before I do anything for you." This
teacher was constantly riding my back, a teacher named
Mr.———, he was a white teacher. I . . . I didn't know
nothing about their prejudice at that time and I was in
that school . . . I was fifteen. He told me, I was walking
through the building, you know, it was time to go home
so I just put my hat on because I had some books in my
hands, you know, and I was fixing them together—he
said, "———, take that hat off." I said, "You say please."
He said: "Who the hell are you asking to say please
to you? I'm a teacher, you don't ask me to say please to
you—I'm your superior." I said, "Is you jiving, man?"
I said . . . I walked away from him and he grabbed me
on my coat. I said, "Okay, I'll take my hat off for you"—

I'm avoiding trouble. I said, "Okay, I'll take my hat off."
He said, "No," he said. "You a wise guy," he said: "you
a wise guy, huh? You one of them black wise guys,
huh?" I said, "You got some nerve, calling me black," I
said. "Okay, I'll pass off here, let me go and I'll go on
home about my business and I'll forget this ever happened." He said, "No, you a wise one. Come on in here."
He took his keys out like, he took his glasses off and put
them in his pocket, he took his watch off and put it on
the table when we got in the room, he closed the room
and the door was locked on the outside. He take his
jacket off and uncuff his sleeves and roll them up. I look
at him and I was standing over there laughing. He
walks up to me and he hit me in the face with a right
hand—he smacked me into stars. I dropped my books.
My mouth flew open wide, I was shocked, surprised, this
teacher hitting me. That teacher in that room, they had
to come in there and get me off that teacher. It took
four of them to come and get me off that teacher.

This same boy, although he has strong racial feelings, is
also more concerned with the behavior of his teachers than
with their race:

. . . I'll tell you the teachers that give a lot of Negro students a hard time in school—I'll tell you—the teachers
that are colored. Them colored teachers, women and male
alike, will give a colored student, whatever school he go
to and every colored teacher in there, he will give the
colored student a hard time if he don't like him. Now the
way a colored teacher approaches students in school, especially if you're a man and he's big and he knows he
can whup you anyway, he'll approach you and he'll tell
you things, and, in "600" schools the teachers tell you, excuse my expression, "I'll whup your ass and I'll beat the
hell out of you, and you must think I'm one of those punk
jitterbugs out there," he said. "Boy, I'll beat your ass like
I'm your so-and-so," and all that jazz. Teachers use that
because they hear it a lot, you know, and a . . . I believe

a lot of teachers got a very low vocabulary. Because of the simple fact that if that's all they know how to tell a student, a student should tell them the same thing.

If a teacher can give a student respect, I tries to give teachers respect. Now, you know when you try and try and try—trying is running out. Your trying runs out. It's just like patience. When you try to have patience with someone and they don't want to get no agreement, they ain't no need of you trying no more.

Another complaint frequently lodged against teachers and other school personnel is that they provide little moral support to the pupil who is experiencing difficulty. Some children view this as personally destructive and can verbalize their experience in rather sophisticated ways, indicating the threat to their self-concept that is involved. One boy expressed his view this way:

BOY:
. . . I left school last week because . . . they bore me . . . not really bore me but they, they, they make me doubt myself, you know, they show me so much to doubt. And the teachers and the deans and all; and all they tell me —"You're not going to pass anything anyway even if you come so I don't know why you're telling me about boycotting." They tell me, my dean told me, he said: "You probably just took the day off. You don't know nothing about boycotting," you know. "You can't even read the signs and whatnot. Your reading is poor and . . . you're not going to get a diploma so I don't know why you even come to school anyway—why do you bother to get up in the morning and come?"

This young man has decided to drop out of school and is convinced he can continue his education more effectively himself. He feels that the school attitude is injurious to his self and carries with it the further danger of making "some dropouts become dropouts in their own life."

. . . but just to think about it, there's something about the schools when they show . . . once you become a dropout or once you look like you're a dropout, they give you so much to doubt, you have no alternative, they knock you the way, they push you the rest of the way. You know?

Once you start this slipping, instead of giving you a hand up, they'll knock you down. This is the way they do it in school as far as I can see. And they have done it . . . they're doing it to me now. . . . Take my dean telling me that I'm not going to make it . . . I couldn't make it . . . there's no use me coming to school anyway. That's doubting me. That's showing me doubt in myself. That's . . . that's not encouraging me to go anywhere. That's not encouraging me to go . . . he's doubting me. He's putting me down. So instead of picking me up he's pushing me down. Actually, that's what he's doing. And that's what makes some dropouts become dropouts in their own life. You know? Education is boss.[6] Like I said, it's very good, but . . . you can make it if you feel, you know, within yourself that you're strong enough to do this. You can make it. And I feel within myself that I'm strong enough to do it. I know, not following anybody out, but I know that if many men that's rich and have what they have today didn't go through no education with this here . . . didn't get any education . . . why can't I do it?

We have seen that some pupils in segregated classrooms view their teachers as denying them education and a sense of personal dignity. Youngsters who have experienced the integrated classroom are aware that the experience does not automatically change the situation for them. Some children, however, regard the integrated classroom as necessarily superior because they believe that the teachers will not allow the same thing to happen to white children as has happened to them and will of necessity expose the whole

[6] "boss" = fine.

class to more learning. A common argument along these lines is expressed by a youngster.

GIRL:

> I mean, some people don't believe in integration but I believe . . . if I have a son when I grow up, if my Tom can sit next to some white man's Dick or Harry, that he can get the same education that they can get because once a white kid's in their class they'll have to raise their class higher up because the white kid will not fall behind because he's so high up. And once a white kid's sitting next to a colored kid—he don't even have to sit next to him, he sit in the back of the room— but that teacher's going to have to teach. And when he teach, you're going to have to learn some way or the other. And that's exactly the way I feel.
>
> Of course, it seems to me, yesterday was my parents' future, today is mine and tomorrow's my kids' . . . and I wouldn't have it half as bad . . . just exactly the way my mother feel. I want my kids to have as she wish hers to have. And I'm going to do everything in my power to make sure they get it.

That the nonsegregated classroom is not automatically more effective in providing improved education for Negro youth is frequently suggested by our informants, who had attended high schools with white and Negro populations. Their comments shed some light on the subtle, often unconscious techniques by which the integrated school may continue the pattern of low achievement by poor Negro youth. As a boy states so poignantly, there are ways in which ". . . you just left out."

BOY:

> Well, it was kind of strange being in the classroom with them . . . they . . . they'd try to like you but it didn't . . . it really didn't do any good in learning. See like this,

when I was going to————. I was in the classroom with
white kids. I mean this doesn't teach you anything. If
you, if you don't know what's what . . . you just left out.
The teacher don't take time for nothing. They tell you,
you know, once they explain, then you come in, they
say . . . well, you just sit there then. That's all, and that
went on . . .

A girl senses that sometimes a teacher "seem like to overlook you" and "wants to shut you off, say like you're not
there or something."

GIRL:
I like my math teacher. He's very nice. He's understanding, but he's hot-tempered. And the rest of my
teachers are so-so, except for my history teacher. He's
a little prejudiced. He doesn't let the Negroes . . . if you
volunteer in class, seems like to overlook you, you know.
Like, he wants to shut you off, say like you're not there
or something like that so that . . . he doesn't want you
to participate in anything. We try to get along. I had
my teacher changed once and then they gave me back
to him.

Some of the youngsters were quick to note any differential
treatment accorded white pupils:

BOY:
Like, take me . . . like, I sit all the way in the back, but
I need glasses. So I tell my teacher, I say: "Can I sit
up in the front? Because I can't see the board." So he
say: "No, no. You want to sit up in the front because
you want to talk to the girls." But like, there's a white
boy in my class named————. He sit about, next to me.
So when he asked the teacher could he sit up in the
front, the teacher said, "Yeah, yeah, you can sit up
front." So when I told him . . . well, I say, "If I can't
sit up in the front, I ain't going to do no work," he just
sent me down to the office and the dean told me, "If you

don't want to work, then you don't want to come to school." So I says, "Why don't you tell the teacher to change my seat to the front?" He say, "Well, a teacher know . . . where the teacher put you, he must have a reason for putting you there." I sits in the back and don't do nothing. I don't copy what's on the board.

The complaints about prejudice did not extend to their classmates. We noticed how one boy felt that it was his teacher's attitude, not his classmates', that affected his achievement. A girl who attended a mixed high school, said:

GIRL:
Oh, we get along very good, Negroes and whites together. we get along very good. Uh, most of the girls are, you know, together. When we're together . . . we hardly see any difference, you know. We never look at the skin color. We just look at each other as a, you know, as a person, as a friend. In school we don't look at each other because she's white and this one is black and you don't say anything about it. We just say she's my friend or that's Mary or Sue or something like that. It makes no difference. We still going to . . . we eat together, we sit together, we have the same classrooms, we go to all the same classrooms, we go to all the classes together. It makes no difference.

These youngsters felt very strongly, however, that white people held stereotyped, negative notions concerning Negroes. Thus several believed integrated education was better so that "the white kids wouldn't think we're such dopes if they could see what we could do."

The fact that these children come to the classroom with a history of lower status, which colors their expectations, has to affect the way in which they perceive the classroom behavior of the teacher. What to the teacher may be thought of as innocent classroom routine, such as matters of seating, calling on students, or homework-checking, may be viewed as having far greater significance by her pupils. What to the teacher may be necessary techniques for handling thirty-five children in a class, five or six times a day, may to her pupils be viewed as exhibiting prejudice and inferior teaching. Large classes in large schools lead to an emphasis on the administrative rather than the educative process. To children dependent upon the schools for the tools for upward mobility, these schools are seen as providing an inadequate preparation.

8. SELF-CONCEPT

THE PARTICIPANTS in the shutdown expressed real and specific grievances against the school system. Perhaps the most significant of the complaints levied against the schools by the informants concerned itself with the negative self-image that school experiences forced upon youngsters, causing some of them to rebel.

The self may be defined as "a composite of thoughts and feelings that constitute a person's awareness of his individual existence, his conception of who and what he is."[1] As a construct, self-concept is drawn from the work of Sullivan, Horney, Mead, and others.[2]

Much has been written concerning the special problems

[1] Arthur J. Jersild, *In Search of Self* (New York: Bureau of Publications, Teachers College, Columbia University, 1960), p. 9.
[2] See George Herbert Mead, *Mind, Self and Society* (Chicago: University of Chicago Press, 1934); Harry Stack Sullivan, *Conceptions of Modern Psychiatry* (Washington, D.C.; William Alanson White Psychiatric Foundation, 1947); Karen Horney, *The Neurotic Personality of Our Time* (New York: W. W. Norton & Co., Inc., 1937); and Eric Homburger Erikson, "The Problem of Ego Identity," *Journal of the American Psychoanalytic Association*, 5, No. 1 (1956), 58-121.

faced by Negroes in America, problems that help create a negative self-image for Negro youth.[3] Most of this literature concerns itself with such social and economic forces as condition of family life, poverty, segregation, and the caste system that preaches that "white is right." Recent study of Negro children has suggested that the literature on this subject may be faulty and that not all Negro children may be burdened with such severely damaged egos as many have believed.[4] If this is so then schools cannot justify their lack of success by pointing to the negative self-images brought by children as a result of overwhelming social and economic problems as the cause of poor school achievement.

- The assumption that negative self-images have prevented Negro children from achieving has prompted one writer to suggest that the schools ". . . have not as yet been used deliberately to change the self-concept of students."[5] Although this may be true, it is also true that interpersonal relations within schools, which consume a major portion of the time and energies of all young people, are constantly affecting the self-concepts of children. For many of our informants a faulty educational system, by not providing for successful experiences and achievement, is itself creating

[3] See, for example, D. Ausubel and Pearl Ausubel, "Ego Development Among Segregated Negro Children," in Harry A. Passow, *Education in Depressed Areas* (New York: Bureau of Publications, Teachers College, Columbia University, 1963), pp. 109-141; Kenneth B. Clark and Mamie P. Clark, "Racial Identification and Preference in Negro Children," in Eleanor E. Maccoby, *et al.*, *Readings in Social Psychology* (New York: Holt, Rinehart and Winston, Inc., 1958), pp. 602-611; and Abram Kardiner and Lionel Ovesey, *The Mark of Oppression: Explorations in the Personality of the American Negro* (Cleveland & New York: The World Publishing Co.), 1957.

[4] David W. Johnson, *Changes in Self and Racial Attitudes of Negro Children Derived from Participation in a Freedom School* (New York: Institute of Urban Studies, Teachers College, Columbia University, 1964), p. 35.

[5] Jean D. Grambs, "The Self-Concept: Basis for Reeducation of Negro Youth," in William C. Kvaraceus, et al., *Negro Self-Concept: Implications for School and Citizenship* (New York: McGraw-Hill Book Co., Inc., 1965) p. 24.

problems of self-concept, making "some dropouts become dropouts in their own lives."

This is not to deny that forces beyond the school's control help shape the personalities of the children attending. Nonetheless, the role of the school itself in shaping the self-concepts of children has received too little attention.

Sociologists and psychologists have long recognized that concepts of self are derived from the behavior of others toward us. The social interaction we have with others is constantly at work to reshape our self-concepts. Although our experience with others can serve to strengthen our egos— our sense of identity—negative experiences can have the opposite effect of injuring the ego.

The potential danger to the individual's sense of self that follows from interaction between persons was recognized by Georg Simmel, when he spoke of the need to maintain reserve and privacy and discretion in our interaction with others. He pointed out that the invasion of the privacy of the other person could be just as violent and morally inadmissible as listening behind closed doors and leering at a stranger's letters.[6]

The need to retain an individual identity apart from others has also been examined in detail by Erving Goffman.[7] He has explored the ways in which persons have maintained privacy and identity in the face of social contacts that operate to destroy the separateness—the very sanity, if you will— of the individual. Goffman speaks of the person as a sacred object, whose sense of worth and significance is threatened by his vulnerability and penetrability. That social interaction poses such a threat to the individual stems from the fact that he has derived his sense of self from others, and

[6] Georg Simmel, *The Sociology of Georg Simmel,* trans. K. H. Wolff (New York: The Free Press, 1950), pp. 307-312.
[7] Erving Goffman, "The Nature of Deference and Demeanor," *American Anthropologist,* 58 (June 1956), 473-502.

unless he is able to develop a stable definition of himself as a separate being, he cannot function as a social being.

If we recognize that schools are dealing with young people who are in the process of developing their self-concepts, we can be more sensitive to those kinds of interaction between persons that occur in schools that are threatening, corrosive, and even blatantly destructive. Some of our informants, although they had never heard of Simmel or Goffman, were clearly able to state the basic problem: "They make me doubt myself."

Before turning to a specific examination of how the school experience can represent an actual threat to the person of the child, we should examine some of the ways in which the conduct of persons toward one another is regulated. Goffman has written of this in some detail. He speaks of the person as a bearer of demeanor and a recipient of deference. Let us turn to an examination of this concept.

By "deference," he means "the appreciation an individual shows another to that other."[8] In other words, by "deference" is meant the image of that individual that others are obliged to express to him in their conduct.

Rules of deference involve all the actors in a social situation. However, the rules may be asymmetrical, and persons in superordinate positions like teachers do have more rights than do persons in subordinate positions like pupils. Yet metaphorical boundaries do exist around the self, and, although the superordinate person can exercise more familiarities, he cannot press too far without creating serious problems for the subordinate persons. In order to maintain distance between the actor and the recipient—a distance that is essential for not violating the "ideal sphere which

---

[8] *Ibid.*, p. 489. For an insightful application of this theory to the slum classroom see G. Alexander Moore, *Urban School Days*, Project TRUE, Hunter College, pp. 111-115.

lies around the recipient"—there are what Goffman has termed avoidance rituals and presentation rituals.

Avoidance rituals refer to the things one should not do. If we recall our informant's complaint that the teacher called her "stupid" because she didn't know the French that the teacher did, we begin to see the dangers to self that arise from the recipient of such behavior's accepting this definition of herself without protest. Appropriate deference on the part of the teacher calls for the avoidance of calling pupils "stupid."

Presentation rituals are things which should be done to define to recipients how they are regarded, for example, salutations, compliments, invitations, and services. We have seen how sensitive to the behavior of their teachers along these lines our informants were. The teacher who avoided giving help, or seating a boy near her, indicated to him her contempt for his self; whereas the teacher who was "patient," who took time to talk and listen and help without denigrating, was spoken of with quiet affection, for the boy's worthiness as a person was being indicated by the teacher's behavior. This teacher did not have to be emotionally involved with the pupil at all—it was her constructive behavior toward him as a student in a situation in which he was supposed to be functioning as a learner that gave him a sense of well-being.

Demeanor, on the other hand, is that element of a person's behavior that sets him up to those in his presence as a person having desirable qualities and being worthy of respect.[9] Demeanor represents socially defined "good manners," which are essential to the establishment of basic trust in any relationship. Our informants were distrustful of teachers who used street language. This kind of manner on the part of the teacher did not strike them as marking the teacher as

9 *Ibid.,* p. 492.

an object worthy of respect. Nor were those teachers who spent much time on what appeared to the pupils as irrelevant humor and personal experiences behaving in the way the pupils expected them to behave as teachers.

Some of our informants were very clearly concerned with the threats to their sense of dignity and self-worth, which came from school situations. These concerns were directed at both overt and covert attacks against their selves. Among the overt attacks that they noted were verbal ones against their intelligence, race, capabilities, manhood, and the like. In addition, there was evidence of invasion of physical privacy as well, intimately related to feelings about self. Thus, kicking, punching, hitting, and frisking all serve as threats against the person.

In addition to the above-mentioned blatant attacks upon self-worth, there is a third area of covert attacks upon individual dignity exerted against all children in school regardless of race. This has to do with all the ineptitude and inadequacies in the educational system itself, which lead to continuous low achievement. Spending a good part of his life within a system, the basic value of which stresses achievement and successful learning, the child, whether Negro or white, who fails or who achieves little is daily confronted with a pernicious corrosion of his sense of self-esteem. Children who are assigned to the slower classes and nonacademic tracks in school have greater problems. Not only are they assigned lower status in school, but their life chances in our economy are lessened. Failure or low academic achievement is rarely interpreted as a teaching failure, as the result of a testing inadequacy, or as a symptom of needed change; rather it is all too often a judgment of the child's incapacity made by the people around him and even by the child himself. For, by what other standards is he to determine his own worth within a school that marks him a failure?

The destructive effect these experiences have upon the person is evident in the reactions of the pupils to these and other frustrating school experiences. Some suffer actual emotional breakdowns. Others react with anger and strike out physically. Still others react—literally in self-protection —by walking out of the situation, becoming truants and dropouts. Others suffer unknown damage to their confidence and internal strength.[10] Others develop strength in directions outside the academic world or via strong peer or family relationships. It is unfortunate that there has been so little empirical research on the destructive role played by interpersonal relations within schools. We hasten to add that for many other children constructive development of self-esteem is going on concurrently, perhaps in the same building or even within the very same classroom. Yet very little research in this area exists to document the differential treatment accorded individuals.[11] Although we give lip service to the notion that the dignity of each child should be respected, the ongoing interpersonal relations and the experiences of the youngsters do not seem to indicate that we really do this at all. Our informants, many of whom suffered the most from denigrating experiences they consciously viewed as threatening to themselves, were the most appreciative of those teachers whose deference and demeanor were such that they did not feel threatened but rather felt themselves strengthened. Patience, politeness, firmness without anger, and attention to the duties of teaching are all viewed with respect.

[10] David Segal, *Frustration in Adolescent Youth* (Washington, D.C.: U.S. Office of Education, 1951), p. 65.
[11] Two notable exceptions: Helen H. Davidson and Gerhard Lang, "Children's Perceptions of their Teacher's Feelings Toward Them Related to Self-Perception, School Achievement and Behavior," *Journal of Experimental Education*, Vol. 29, No. 2 (December 1960); and *Study of Social and Psychological Processes in the Classroom*, Bank Street College of Education School and Mental Health Program, unpublished report.

We may ask, "What of the other side of the coin?" What about those teachers thrust into situations where children with difficult behavior patterns and antagonistic attitudes confront the teacher with demeanor and deference patterns that attack *their* selves? We recognize that this happens and in some cases may indeed be the precipitating factor in the kinds of negative teacher behavior our informants described.

Until very recently few teachers or their supervisors were deliberately educated or inspired to grasp the problems of people in depressed, color-confined neighborhoods or to appreciate their aspirations and understand their culture.[12] Thus many dedicated, well-meaning individuals have been thrust into situations for which they are unprepared by traditional teacher training. In addition to the factor of inadequate preparation for their difficult task, teachers are prone to identify with upper-income groups.[13] Many such persons find it difficult to accept lower-class children—this appears to be as true for Negro teachers as for whites—unless they outwardly conform to the values of their teachers. In addition, some white teachers find it difficult to empathize with Negro children, regardless of class.

Complicating the situation is the fact that many teachers have been thrust into situations in which they are expected to cope with too many factors at once—among them class size, inexperience, lack of adequate professional supervision to ensure successful teaching,[14] and lack of skill, facilities, auxiliary assistance, and so forth.

[12] National Defense Education Act Institutes were among the first efforts in this regard.

[13] Howard S. Becker, "The Career of the Chicago School Teacher," *American Journal of Sociology*, 57 (March 1952), 470-477.

[14] Inadequate supervision rather than teacher inexperience has been cited by the HARYOU Report as the major factor in the low achievement of Central Harlem youngsters; see *Youth in the Ghetto* (New York: Harlem Youth Opportunities Unlimited, 1964), p. 220.

The beginning teacher especially needs assistance in these directions, for she is extremely vulnerable in her relations with her pupils, just as they are vulnerable in their relations with her. She is faced with attacks upon her self-worth that come with failing to do her job as she had expected; her nonachieving pupils confront her with the fact of her failure daily; she is also faced with physical invasion of her privacy by children who push, shove, and hit; and she is subject to verbal assaults as well, in the form of cursing, profanity, and verbal attacks on her integrity—for example, "you don't teach," or "you can't teach." She, too, may react in self-defense by use of physical punishment, by verbal assault, or by breaking down, by seeking a transfer or simply by quitting, becoming one of the teacher "dropouts."

It may be argued that morale is directly related to the ability of individuals within the system to function successfully in the roles that have ideally been established for them. If pupils are to learn, the school must make it possible for them to learn successfully by creating the teaching situations in which each individual is treated in ways that strengthen his sense of self-worth, his sense of dignity. Without this, we must expect deviant behavior and/or personal breakdown.[15] These problems affect teachers as well as pupils, but the pupils are the most vulnerable, for they are still children, and the educational experience for them is critical in determining their future positions in society.

CLASS DIFFERENCES IN GETTING THROUGH THE SYSTEM

Many of the problems faced by these children may also be faced by children of all social classes who do not succeed academically in school. The need to provide for the self-esteem and dignity of all children is likely to grow as the hold-

[15] Kvaraceus, *op. cit.,* p. 109.

ing power of American public schools increases to include more slow learners and reluctant learners than ever before in history, regardless of class or race.

On the whole, however, middle-class children are more successful than lower-class Negro and white children in moving through the school system. This stems from the availability of mechanisms that exist to assist the former. It is commonly heard that "the child learns in spite of the teacher or the school," and there are two ways of looking at this. One suggests that the achievement stems from some innate drive on the part of the child; the other supposes that supportive mechanisms in the family, community, or the institution of the school itself exist to ensure success. In actuality, all may be related, in that the child's drive may stem from a confidence in the possibility of success— confidence that is fed by the mechanisms we shall examine.

A significant aspect of this is the expectation by all—family, the child himself, school, peers—that the child will succeed. Barring the most severe handicaps, whether physical, mental, or emotional, the child finds support in his movement through school from various sources. His own self-concept, plus his parental and peer support, operates to help him. The school assumes he will learn and provides concern and programs for his progress. There exists a whole complex of mechanisms whereby this self-fulfilling prophecy is assured of its completion.[16]

Middle-class parents sometimes find themselves dissatisfied with those experiences their children have in the public schools that they see as interfering with the children's

---

[16] For a discussion of the self-fulfilling prophecy as it applies to Negroes in a negative direction, see Robert K. Merton, *Social Theory and Social Structure*, rev. ed. (New York: The Free Press, 1957), pp. 421-436; Clark, *Dark Ghetto* (New York: Harper & Row, 1965), pp. 127-129; Gunnar Myrdal, *An American Dilemma* (New York: Harper & Row, 1944), pp. 75-78; and R. M. MacIver, *The More Perfect Union* (New York: The Macmillan Co., 1948), pp. 52-81.

chances for successful futures. That middle-class parents too are losing control over the management of their children is discussed by Aaron V. Cicourel and John I. Kitsuse in *The Educational Decision-Makers*.[17] Increasingly the autonomy and authority of the school system over the children within it, insofar as class placement and "tracking" of students is concerned, have limited the influence of all parents. Nonetheless, Cicourel and Kitsuse see the school as continuing to favor the middle and upper social classes:

> . . . we suggest that the influence of social class upon the way students are processed in the high school today is reflected in new and more subtle family-school relations than the direct and often blatant manipulation of family class pressure documented by Hollingshead. In one sense, the influences of social class on the treatment accorded students has become a built in feature of the organizational activities of the modern comprehensive high school, particularly those with highly developed counseling programs. Insofar as the high school is committed to the task of identifying talent and increasing the proportion of college-going students, counselors will tend to devote more of their time and activities to those students who plan and are most likely to go to college, and whose parents actively support their plans and make active inquiries at the school about their progress—namely, the students from the middle and upper social classes.[18]

In an effort to counteract the loss of control over the schools' handling of their children, middle-class parents utilize compensatory mechanisms to help ensure their children's success. One of these ways is through the availability of supportive tutoring that can be purchased.

These tutoring services cater largely to two extremes of

[17] Aaron V. Cicourel and John I. Kitsuse, *The Educational Decision-Makers* (Indianapolis & New York: Bobbs-Merrill Co., Inc., 1963).
[18] *Ibid.*, p. 145. It should be noted that the authors are referring to college counseling.

youth able to afford their services. At one extreme are those who are in danger of failing in their academic work. At the other are those who wish to ensure very high grades in order to meet the tremendous competition for entrance into the most prestigious colleges.

Indeed, it is a possibility that the schools, although superior in facilities, are not always superior in the teaching offered to children in middle-class areas. Many children in such schools achieve well but not necessarily because of the training provided within the school itself. Tremendous supportive action by families is often required to ensure achievement at the level expected by teachers, families, and the children themselves.

Evidence of this is to be found in an examination of the parents' bulletins of schools in higher-income areas. A review of such bulletins in New York City, including one from one of the most academically selective high schools in the country, reveals an inordinate amount of advertising by tutoring services. Such ads read:

Private tutor—Spanish, Algebra, Geometry, years of experience, summer tutoring also

Professional Tutoring Service. All subjects—all grades— all tutoring by qualified licensed teachers and Department Chairmen in your home

Don't wait for Exams—Get the right start now—individual instruction

Math tutoring—excellent results in Regents

Math specialist—individualized approach—improved study skills

Mother and Dad: If your children need help in school— Do Not Neglect Them—Let us restore their confidence by sending a professional Teacher to your home. Helping to Bring Them up to Grade—all subjects—Mid-Term and Final Exams

*Parents: Is Your Youngster Doing As Well As He Should
In School?*—*Private tutoring at home, all subjects.*

Large numbers of college-board review courses are also offered. One bulletin issued by a parents' association listed
eighteen ads for tutoring out of a total of nineteen.

Most of the tutoring services are provided by teachers
and department chairmen who work in the schools but who
augment their incomes by private tutoring. Because of their
familiarity with school requirements, examinations, and
procedures, they facilitate academic adjustment for those
who can afford their services. Fees range from $6 per hour
for a group class to $12 per hour for individual instruction.

Not the least significant factor surrounding this tutoring
is the familiarity on the part of the tutors with how to handle
school requirements. (That there are serious inequities that
can result from this is attested by the Board of Education
ruling that teachers may not sell tutoring services to pupils
who attend the specific schools in which they teach, a ruling many circumvent.) Another way in which middle-class
parents express their dissatisfaction and ensure successful
schooling for their children is by moving into neighborhoods
or suburbs where they consider the schools better or by
totally removing their children and placing them in private
schools.[19]

Also, middle-class parents, both white and Negro, have
made their influence felt through their parents' associations.
Sometimes this is done in the form of direct action to
improve school conditions by raising funds for such improved facilities as libraries or audiovisual aids, thus sup-
plementing the public assistance given education by the
state, or by political pressure for higher budgets. The parents' associations, however, also enable some parents to
familiarize themselves with the school routine in order to

[19] Over 450,000 New York City children attend private or parochial school.

help their children or in order to establish more personal contact with administrators and teachers to assure more active concern for their particular children. Some mothers even manage to be present physically in the classroom rather frequently, acting in the role of "class mother," or assistant to the teacher.

Still another mechanism operates to enable the middle-class parent to exert watchfulness over the school's handling of his child. Through residence in the same neighborhood, through friends, relatives, and religious organizations, the middle-class parent is in a position to know a teacher in the local school personally, or a friend of the teacher, or some staff member. Because of these contacts, a child's problems can be examined personally and sympathetically, and the solution facilitated.

That the middle class is not entirely happy with the work of the schools results in pressures directed against schools to ensure success for their children. Many school principals and teachers shy away from the middle-class-area school, fearful of the "pampering," the "pushing," and the "complaining" parents with whom they have to deal. The complaining parents in these situations are often those with similar sociocultural backgrounds to those of the school staff, sometimes with superior education or higher income and able to "speak the same language." Their protests, though annoying, are nonetheless conducted in socially acceptable ways and appear dignified to the school.

Pressures are exerted by parents on children to attain high marks. Sometimes differential marking occurs within schools and between schools. An instance of alleged deliberate falsification of grades by school personnel to ensure entry into the Ivy League was recently raised by Yale University.

The lower-class parent has few of the above-mentioned resources and techniques available to him. Indeed, the school is considered to be responsible for teaching the child; when the child fails, the parent unfamiliar with the structure and mechanisms of formal, urban education is more likely to blame the child or to accept his inability, because the techniques for getting the child through the system are less familiar to the parent, and the personnel operating the schools are more distant. Although parents' associations do exist, they tend to attract those individuals who are already upwardly mobile and who seek to develop the techniques of working with the system, to help move their children. In lower-class, minority-group neighborhoods, the parents' associations have always had limited memberships.

In addition, class differences in teacher reactions to pupils have been noted in the areas of teaching procedures, discipline, and moral acceptability. Lower-class pupils often fail to live up to the teacher's concept of the ideal pupil and thereby do not compare favorably with the upper classes.[20]

We have seen that, in recent years, the civil-rights movement, plus a growing awareness that unemployment is heaviest for those without formal schooling at least through the high-school level, has begun to activate some lower-class parents, as well as upwardly mobile minority-group parents, who see the schools functioning to bar their children from acquiring the needed skills for full equality. Direct confrontation with the schools in the form of boycotts is their way of seeking changes in the direction of a better future for their children. The techniques are not those used by the middle class, but they seek to achieve the same purpose: some control over what society, through the structure of the school, is doing with their children. They see the schools as not providing their children with the essential training for equal competition for positions in the larger society.

[20] Becker, "Social Class Variations in the Teacher-Pupil Relationship," *Journal of Educational Sociology*, 25 (April 1952), 451-465.

9. CONFRONTATION WITH THE LAW

IT IS CLEAR that the participants we interviewed had serious complaints to levy against the schools. Previous to the shutdown, however, they had not protested in any organized way. The boycott provided training in the exercise of social pressure. It was, in a sense, an exercise in the use of power.

Many of the boys and girls attracted to the freedom schools and to the picket lines were extremely uncomfortable concerning the possible illegality of their actions. The fears they had grew out of the expectation of reprisals from various sources. Many, who were not dropouts or failures in academic work, were afraid of falling behind or being failed in school. In answer to this came the argument: "You see, I want a better education. I say, if you stay out boycotting for that for a month, well, it's nothing compared to your whole education." In addition, the Charter Group for a Pledge of Conscience, working with the Harlem Parents Committee and the Parents' Workshop in Brooklyn, provided tutorial assistance to those children who, upon returning to school, found themselves in danger of failing.

Others, out of school without the permission of their parents or guardians, were afraid of what their families would do to them if they were found out. Many gave false names and addresses to the people in charge of the freedom schools. Some, while on picket lines, were heard to say, "My old lady would beat my head if she saw me here." Indeed, there were reports of parental beating of children when attendance officers returned some youngsters to their homes. Apparently, however, many did not fear parental reprisals. When the director of the Manhattan freedom school announced that she was sending letters home informing families that their children had been in attendance in the school, youngsters offered their correct names and addresses.

The boys and girls asked for reassurance from the teachers concerning the possibility of legal reprisals for their actions. They were told by freedom school leaders that their strength lay in numbers and that the schools probably would not fail large blocs of children or punish large numbers for illegal truancy.

Indeed, the significance of absence as a weapon was taught, for the teachers explained the fact that the New York City Board of Education receives funds in accordance with *per diem* attendance. "Man, that's cool," came the response, as the point was understood that their absence was felt by school authorities in a very direct way.

When the supervising attendance officer appeared at the Riverside Church to talk to the assembled teen-agers present, he urged them to return to school. He told them that there would be no penalties if they returned; if they didn't, they would be violating the law and be subject to penalties. He asked the assembled pupils to rise and follow him. The leaders of the freedom school were quite unprepared for what followed. In response to his appeal, all the students, including the well behaved and the disruptive, sat silently, until there came from the audience the song, quickly picked up by all the others, "We Shall Not Be Moved."

The freedom school at Siloam Presbyterian Church made an effort to get parental consent for those attending. Here, too, the boys and girls were not at first prepared to connect their absence with legal reprisals. This lack of awareness was expressed by one girl, who was surprised by her confrontation with the law during picketing of the Board of Education:

GIRL:

. . . I have to tell you what happened—this story will amaze you. We're walking down the street, you know, opposite the Board of Education, and a truant officer, I think, no it was a cop arrested this boy that was walking along with me. And so I turn around and I say something to him, you know, and I seen the cop there and I said: "What's the matter, what'd you do? You didn't do nothing." So the truant officer comes up to me and says, "Do you want to go to jail?" I smiled at him because, you know, I really thought he was playing, you know, smiled and everything was pleasant and he say all right, get in the car. I says: "Look, I didn't do nothing. I'm walking down the street and I'm not getting in that car unless I did something." All these, I mean, one little old me—all these cops and truant officers would grab me and drag me to the ground and threw me in the car and everything and then when they got down to court you should hear some of the lies that come out. I'm down there for a . . . at first I thought I was being down there for walking the street. When you get down there, I'm for assault and battery, this all . . . of resisting arrest, trespassing, and a couple other thousand things thrown in. I says, "What's this?" I do not . . . here I'm charged with all this jazz, you know, and you just should seen the way those cops brought those grown-ups in. They lift kids by our clothes, you know, and they drag you and it's just disgusting. There's nothing glamorous in getting arrested, I'll tell you that much.

One boy gang leader, experienced in much antisocial behavior, still feared direct confrontation with the law on a social-protest issue. He described the depth of feeling involved in a decision to take his place on the picket line:

BOY:
And, you know, inside, you know, I was scared. You know, I said now if I was to go down here, I said, I never been on nothing like that before, you know. So after that everybody went home. We didn't go no places. That was the first couple days I was coming down here —about three days—and the fourth day is the time we went.

So I went home that night and I was thinking to myself. I said—I want my kids to come up honest and clean and with a good education because I plan on getting a good one myself. I said they might start out like I do but I don't want them to wind up like I do, you know. I want them to have a good education and things. So, I was saying, thinking very hard. So I went home that night and I was just thinking, thinking to myself, you know . . . and I lay in the bed, you know, before I go to sleep and I think to myself, and I was thinking so hard that I had a dream about it. And I was thinking that— now if I go downtown—I was just, you know, just thinking, and I was saying to myself that I want my kids to grow up, you know, in a decent school and a decent neighborhood. So I was thinking . . . I was thinking about whether to say yes or no to————about going downtown or anyplace. So I said, "Oh, I'll go ahead and do it." I said, "It won't kill me and if I do die I'll die trying . . ."

This boy, despite his stance as a leader, was nonetheless very wary of his new role in civil-rights agitation. He had fought local gang enemies in the neighborhood park and had beat up a teacher, but these activities were not nearly so difficult as the decision to picket the Board of Education. To make that decision, he reflected very seriously concerning himself and his future.

Although Reverend Galamison had attempted some preparation of the children for confrontation with the police, greater dependence was placed upon the adult leadership for maintaining decorum on the picket lines. The children were not well trained in matters of behavior during acts of civil disobedience.

This lack of careful preparation for the handling of provocations, plus the arrest by the police of those adults who were supervising the picket lines before the Board of Education offices, resulted in outbreaks that were headlined by the metropolitan press as "riots." These "riots" were provoked in part by St. John's University students who shouted, "Niggers, go home." Although greater training in civil disobedience might have averted difficulty, the unprepared, unsupervised youngsters reacted in a volatile manner:

GIRL:
Then, you know, we went down to the picket lines . . . oh, I hated it, down there. But, you know, when you're down on the picket lines you have to learn how to take everything from people—you have to listen to people talk about you. And most teen-agers . . . you know, when people say something about . . . they'll want to jump up and fight. But you'd be amazed that all of us around here are peaceful and everything and . . . Those white students from St. John's University had to say, "Niggers, go home." Now, all of us all riled up because they had arrested all the adults and some of the teen-agers that tried to take over when the grown-ups had gone . . .

every time one of the kids tried to get order they'd arrest him or something like that. And when those St.
John's University students, they said, "Niggers, go
home," and everybody just exploded and it was disgusting.

And then, everytime, it seemed like when you want
to get a little, a little room to do something, those cops
would push you back. Now, they're telling you to keep
moving but yet they're pushing you back and everything.
I was trying to talk to some of these white people—
they had just got on the picket line and this horse chased
me up and down the street.

One picket-line captain, a teen-ager himself, described his
arrest:

BOY:
I kept them in a straight line and in order. Then when
it was time to go home, I'd tell them to follow me and
things like that. The police officers, they took me out
from the line and said I was influencing kids to stay out
of school.

Without supervision, the youngsters themselves were unprepared to exercise self-discipline in the face of opposition.
Thus, many fought the police, as well as the students who
called them "niggers."

GIRL:
And everytime we would go down town and demonstrate
they would arrest all the adults and they would leave
us, you know, without any adult supervision. Then they
would run behind us with horses and nightsticks and
whatnot. And the boys would become angry, then they
would fight back like the time they knocked————out.
A cop . . . they had, they had us inside a barricade and
the kids were marching around and————got pushed
into the barricade and one of the cops knocked him out.
His heart beat twice and he fell down. And then the

boys became mad and they started fighting, you know, fussing with the cops back and forth. There's some boys from St. John's University who came up to the edge of the parking lot and said, "Niggers, go home." And then the boys chased them and they started fighting.

Although Reverend Galamison had urged that there be discipline and had warned against drinking, he did not have enough time with these youngsters or enough help from experienced civil-rights demonstrators to control all those who followed him:

BOY:
Before we went downtown and we went down there . . . I had a little drink. And I . . . we went down there and a cop did something to somebody and we started with the cops. And the cops started chasing us and everything and we was running all over downtown and breaking windows.

Although the police arrested very few of the participants, they did arrest the leaders of the picket line, thus creating the situation in which the undisciplined, unprepared to handle taunts and insults nonviolently, reacted in a volatile manner. The actual damage consisted of one serious injury to a Negro boy and several broken windows. There was no looting.

One boy described his belief that greater discipline was necessary:

BOY:
. . . you can't just go down, you just can't go down here and take a whole bunch of children with you, I mean without them being rowdy and everything, and go out there and have somebody walk around and after they finish walking around then they come on home. You can't do that without them making a whole lot of noise. I don't think it's right. Because if I was a cop, you know,

I'd throw them all in jail . . . now that's the difference between the boycotts up here and the boycotts down there [in Selma]. You see they went down there and they knew how to act, you see, because they're probably, they're probably accomplishing what they wanted to accomplish but, see, we, all the time we was boycotting up here we didn't accomplish what we was supposed, what they, what everybody wanted, see. So the march in Selma was better, a whole lot better than the one in Brooklyn.

Those boys and girls who prior to the boycott were already involved in the civil-rights movement in New York City were deeply committed to solidarity with the efforts of southern Negroes to achieve civil rights. They saw their own agitation for better schooling as allied to that movement and as part of the national movement to gain equality for Negroes in American society. For the youngsters who had had no previous involvement with the civil-rights movement before this shutdown, the experiences they had talking with others and discussing these problems in the freedom schools led to increased awareness.

The civil-rights march in Selma, Alabama, in the spring of 1965, was being headlined by the press several weeks after the shutdown ended. In our discussions with the youngsters we found there was unanimous support for the Selma action. Several children active in the civil-rights movement in New York City had even gone to Selma.

GIRL:
It's really nice. And I felt so sorry, you know because when I went down to Selma . . . I don't know, I didn't like it down there so I came back. You know, it's just disgusting down there . . . you don't really know. It's like another world down there, it really is . . . it's just another world down . . . it's not even part of the United States down there. I don't know, it's just . . . I don't like

. . . New York is bad enough, but Selma! . . . I firmly back it. If I had money, if I had anything and they wanted me to donate I'd give everything I had because . . . they really need it. They need help down there. They need all the people they can get because what they believe in is true and it's firm and it's a good belief.

They viewed the Selma march to Montgomery and the proposed economic boycott of Alabama suggested by Martin Luther King, Jr., with sympathy and wished to participate. All saw the demonstration in Selma as clearly related to their own actions in New York—both being viewed as related to the struggle for equal rights.

BOY:

I think it is a good thing. I think the boycott even be better, you know, stopping trade, stop trading with them, for us I think that would be better. The President would know that the Negroes really want their rights. And if everybody should do it, it's not only the Negroes interested in it, the Negroes over in Selma, it's everybody else that's interested in it. Everybody should have equal rights.

INTERVIEWER:

Do you think that if you were in Selma that you would have joined . . . ?

BOY:

Yep. I wanted to go, but . . . no cash.

An appraisal of the possibility of rapid success for full equality was also made, and these children did not delude themselves into expectations of miraculous changes occurring rapidly.

BOY:

Because, like say in Selma . . . in Selma it was the vote —they won't let too many Negroes vote; in New York it's the schools; and different things in other places. That's why they in one place trying to do what it takes

them about three or four years before they finally get
that settled and then they have to go to another place
and they're ignored for about two or three years until
they start demonstrating and picketing schools and all
that. And they keep on really going quite a long time
before . . . it might be, you know, everybody will just
one day . . . everybody have the same rights, everybody
get the same education. But I don't think it'll be coming
. . . it won't happen before the next twenty years are
up.

Their growing perception that the struggle against *de
facto* segregation in New York City was part of the na-
tionwide struggle for full equality caused some of these
youngsters to display impatience with their fellows who did
not share their views concerning the importance of the local
fight. In some cases the youngsters attempted to share their
realization with classmates who did not participate in the
shutdown:

GIRL:
   . . . our guidance teacher let us discuss Negro history
   one day. So he asked the kids a question, he said, "If
   you were, if you had all the qualifications to vote and
   you were old enough to vote, would you have joined the
   march down in Selma?" And everyone stood up and
   said yes. Yet the majority of the kids in my class didn't
   participate in the boycott and didn't go on any demonstrations. So I raised my hand and asked the chairman,
   "Can I have the floor?" And I asked them just for record how many of them, would they raise their hands,
   the ones that said they would go down to Selma and
   march and practically all the class they raised their
   hands. So I told them how in the world could they say
   that they would go down to Selma and march and they
   wouldn't march right up here and fight for theirselves?
   . . . I said, don't hand no one no junk like that saying
   you would go to Selma, because, I said, because it

doesn't make any sense. If you have enough . . . it's worse down with Selma than it is up here because they can go around bombing and get away with things like that. The cops up here do the same thing but they're kind of slick with it. And if you can go down South and face guns and hoses and things like this, why can't you just come up here and, and demonstrate? And they, everybody wants to go to Selma but nobody wants to do nothing about up here.

INTERVIEWER:

Would you go to Selma?

GIRL:

My mother wouldn't let me go but if I was on my own I would have went.

Another girl, a very successful academic student, felt so deeply about the Negro's position in American life, that she reacted with great sadness to the lack of understanding on the part of her Negro classmates:

GIRL:

. . . Girls ask me in school—What is the boycott for? What does it mean? What does integration mean? What is segregation?—and I don't, I don't know. I just didn't see any sense in telling them I just got so fed up. Sixteen- and seventeen-year-old girls asking me that! I didn't even, I wouldn't tell them. I just walked away. . . . Just about all the white students knew. A lot of white girls from my school participated in it too. But for a Negro to get up and ask me, "What, what does integration mean or segregation or ghetto neighborhood?" . . . something like that—it made you feel very bad. I didn't answer them. I just kept on walking . . . a lot of girls asked me why did I participate in it? But the majority of the girls, they acted as if nothing had happened, you know, just as . . . we were friends, we're still friends but, I don't know, each time we talk about civil rights they seemed like they were getting farther and farther away.

One of the reasons for this same girl's participation in the shutdown was the need to affirm her solidarity with the civil-rights struggle in the South. She, too, viewed her actions in New York as related to the larger national struggle:

GIRL:
> Well, my mother was for the boycott but for me to stay home, and the day for me to be in the boycott, she didn't want me to be in it at all. She didn't mind me going and helping and everything but she thought it was taking up too much of my school time or my school work. And she figured that, maybe, you know, I'd lack credits or my marks would drop, down or something. We talked about it for a long time. We talked about it and we just straightened it out, you know. And so, I guess, she, she understood, she understood why I did it because I know I told her that, I don't know, if I didn't participate in the boycott I just wouldn't feel right. All the Negroes down South are trying to get freedom, trying to vote, trying to go to better schools and here I am up in the city and I can go to a good school and I can get a good education, not the best, but it's good, it's better than there . . . and they can't, they can't get any. So I figured if I couldn't be in it then I didn't see any reasons why I should go to school and try to get an education when they couldn't get one at all. So she understood it and she said it was all right . . .

Her view of the Negro problem caused this same girl some difficulties in school, where her teacher was unprepared to cope with her depth of feeling. The following incident is typical of some that lead teachers to consider pupils "arrogant"; yet it may be unrealistic for the schoolteacher to expect this girl to engage in polite discussion on an issue in which she is so thoroughly involved. Nor does the teacher's handling of the situation indicate awareness on his part of the positive aspects involved in this girl's ability to argue with a white opponent.

GIRL:

The teacher asked a question about Alabama. "Why do you think the Negroes are boycotting for their votes? Why did it take them so long to start and why didn't they start, you know, sometime back further?" And the girl raised her hand and, she was a white girl. She was from down South. And she said that she thought they shouldn't fight for their rights, that they should wait and they should go back to Africa where they came from. And we got in an argument and I told her that they waited long enough, you know. It's time for them to wake up now. They've been waiting for a hundred years and it's about time that they started doing something.

And then the teacher told me to sit down and be quiet and he told me I didn't raise my hand. I should raise my hand before I spoke. And I said I thought I was entitled to speak because nobody else was speaking and you didn't object to her when she started speaking. So I don't see why you should object to me. And he went on and talked about I didn't have any manners, that I should do this or I should do that and I didn't feel like listening to him, so he told me to get out of the classroom.

And so I got out—I got my coat and got out, walked up, so he said don't come back until you get your mother. So I said, "Well, that's fine with me because I wasn't coming back anyway because you don't teach in your class." He just turned red—he got very angry. But then I didn't say it that way, you know, the way I . . . that's the way I surmise the whole thing up.

INTERVIEWER:

What happened? Did you bring your mother back?

GIRL:

No, I went there, back to the class Tuesday but I went downstairs and told the dean and she wrote a note out.

. . . She wants me to get out of the class, you know. She wants to put me in another history class. I think I . . . I'm going to stay in that one that I'm in now because if you go it just looks like you're running and I don't like to run. So I just stay where I'm at.

INTERVIEWER:

What about the other students in school, the other girls? How do they feel about this particular situation?

GIRL:

Oh, well, some girls in the class . . . they won't talk up in front of the class but, you know, when you get outside and you know how the girls are going to talk and say well, "You shouldn't of done this and you shouldn't of done that," and a lot of girls they just don't say anything. I was the only one that said anything about it in classroom. And when I got outside they told me, they said, "Well, you shouldn't have done it and you shouldn't have done this." Now I . . . to me it seems so silly that if you know something is wrong and you don't say something about it, the teach . . . he's going to either think you don't care, you're stupid, or something. And if you don't open your mouth and say it he's not going to know. So I just told them and, I mean, if he didn't like it it was just too bad because it was said and I wasn't going to take it back. I didn't care.

10. WHAT THEY LEARNED

ARLIER it was noted that conflict functions to reduce social isolation and unite individuals and groups otherwise unrelated or even antagonistic to one another in a common struggle. Another function of conflict is to serve, once the groups and associations have been formed, to maintain boundary lines between them and the surrounding social environment, by assigning positions to the various subgroups within the system and by helping to define the power relations among them.[1] This function of conflict was recognized by New York State Commissioner of Education Allen who said that both PAT and Reverend Galamison served to sharpen the issues confronting the educational system. The youngsters interviewed were better able, because of their experience, to comprehend their status and roles in school and society with increased understanding. They had a clearer view of who they were and where they

[1] Lewis Coser, *The Functions of Social Conflict* (New York: The Free Press, 1956), p. 155.

were. Also, as several of the informants indicated, they drew boundaries between themselves and nonparticipants.

The growing awareness of their roles as Negro Americans seeking pride in themselves and groping for equality in society was one of the most significant aspects of the boycott experience.

As confidence in their new roles developed, several youngsters began to write poetry and song lyrics to buoy up the courage of their fellows. Two ninth graders attending the freedom school at the Riverside Church composed "Picket Line Blues." Written February 23, 1965, it urged: "Don't walk on by, / don't walk on by, / don't walk on by, / Come in and sympathize."

Picket Line Blues
by Stanley Dickerson and
Reggi Harris
Harlem Youth Committee

If you see the tears rolling
    down my eyes,
Don't let me be, come on and
    sympathize.
When you see what the white man's
    doing to me,
You know it's because he doesn't
    want me free.
        Don't walk on by, don't walk on by,
           don't walk on by,
        Come in and sympathize.
You know he's scared to let me
    have my rights,
But he knows damn well we're gonna
    win this fight.
What he doesn't know is that
    only when we're free,
It's not til then he'll be
    equal to me.

One fourteen-year-old girl, an active leader in Brooklyn, wrote:

Fighters of Macon!
Are You Black Like Me?

By Thelma Sutherland

Are you Black like me?
Black from your head to your feet?
Are you sorry because you're you?
Don't be, because there's others in this boat too.

Are you Puerto Rican direct from the slum?
Because we desire freedom are we bums?
Because we need and must get our goal,
Integration forever to have and to hold.

We are members of the human race,
My skin is black and I won't wear a veil over my face.
I'm proud so very proud of what I am and can be,
Freedom is my chief desire, yes indeed!

Don't be ashamed of yourself, never, never,
There is no need so don't you ever.
There is one way freedom can be gained,
To stand up and state your game.

The white can jail—kill me too,
But freedom must live on and never be doomed.
Freedom is what's really happening today,
If you want freedom stop this way.

I'm a Macon Fighter from Herkimer Court.
My freedom won't be sold or bought.
Are you with me or are you not?
If so on with the February 3 boycott!

In addition to the growing awareness of themselves and social issues, the boycott experience led to increasing responsibility on the part of many. One of the more significant aspects of the boycott in Brooklyn, for example, was that

leaders of juvenile gangs, some of which were known to
have engaged in serious antisocial acts—like intergang violence and terror in local parks at night—suppressed their
tendencies to fight with one another. The former head of
one of the more notorious gangs of the area emerged as a
constructive leader in this respect. He was able to channel
the aggressive tendencies of the various cliques and gangs
who had been attracted to the "action" at the church during
the period of the boycott. Many of these boys were already
truants and were drawn to the church as word spread
throughout the borough concerning the events going on.
The boy leader describes what happened:

BOY:
> Oh, the first day I came here they was in here and it
> was, it was me and my boys down here. See this is our
> territory. It was like this here with the boycott—every-
> body was fighting. Everybody was fighting. We was
> fighting among ourselves. Boys got into fights, girls got
> into fights and then one day me . . . see, now, it kind of,
> see, excuse my expression but we were . . . we ganged
> down here, you know. I'm not jitterbugging no more,
> I'm not a member of the gang—I used to be a member
> of the gang, I used to be vice-president of the Chaplains
> from ——— Avenue, then we broke up because we fig-
> ured that, you know, at the age of 16 and 17 all that's in
> the past, you know. We felt that we had outgrown all
> that jitterbugging. Some boys still have it in their mind.
> Now me, I don't. What I'm out for is I'm out for a
> honest buck and a clean living, you know. So I, we was
> down here and we, they're fighting, and then one day
> me and my boys . . . see this is known as our territory,
> you know . . . they had boys here from Stuyvesant Ave-
> nue, ———, and ———, all boys from Brownsville and
> Bushwick Projects and boys from all over Brooklyn,
> mostly Bed-Stuy. And this is our section and there was
> seven of us up there—there's a good number of my boys

up there. And we got up on the stage and we got everybody quiet. . . . There was still some little wise-guys in
the crowd so we just went down on the stage, on the
floor and we just told them to shut up or else get out.
So they kept quiet and we was talking with them.
We told them, "Why should we fight among ourselves
when we got the boycott?" . . . We, I told them, I says,
"See Mr.———, Miss———, Miss———, Mrs.———
. . . all of them are some very nice people, all of them
. . . all the people that's in the CORE I think are very
nice." And I told them, and Reverend Galamison, he's
a very nice man also. I believe all those people are very
good people . . . good people is what I consider them.
And, we was talking and I said, "You all making it hard
on them to handle us," I said. "In order for us to win
what we're fighting for, *we* got to work together, you
know, like the UN, be united." United Negroes is what
we call it, you know. So we, everybody started talking
and we got the group leaders together and we just got
a agreement that there'll be no more fighting and we
was working with each other. So, so I feel after, after
everybody got negotiated, then was the, then came the
big steps. ———told me and my boys, he said, "If we
can get these people here together, we can go downtown
to the Board of Education, the Department of Health,
the City Hall . . ."

The boys and girls we interviewed were very articulate
concerning what they believed they had learned from the
boycott experience. Perhaps the most significant thing
pointed to was the tremendously good feeling that came with
being part of a group concerned with their problems. For
many this was an exciting experience. Another aspect to
which our informants pointed was the understanding they
gained concerning other people and their different opinions
of things. One is struck with the ability to empathize,

though disagreeing, that these young people displayed. Greater awareness of the world, their place in it, and their relationship as individuals to larger social problems was evident. In addition, and perhaps most significant, many of these youngsters were for the first time asked to do something that they could see as useful. It gave many of them a real sense of pride.

To one fourteen-year-old girl, the boycott participation meant that ". . . it teach you a little bit of humanity . . .":

GIRL:
It seems like, you know, when you're in a freedom school and you're with a lot of kids that have the same problem and you understand them more, it's so much better for you because when I got back to school it seems like I understood people more and why some of us couldn't get ahead of others and everything. It was real nice. I think it teach you a little bit of humanity and everything. It's real great. . . . I learned to understand people, I mean my problems, and I learned which way you have to turn when you in need. . . . I love school, I mean, it's a nice place where it's nice and quiet there and you can go into solitary or whatever you want to do there. But, out on the streets where you have to face reality, it's just great out there when you, there's a lot of Negro kids out there and they understand the same problems or you is in the same boat or you going out to get your freedom. It's just great. Oh, brother . . . . I don't like to talk, I really don't. But, you know, when you're in that freedom school, and everybody's sharing the same problem, you can get up on that stage and not care if there's a thousand people watching you . . . you just can get up there and talk because your heart is so full and you know what you're talking about . . . because I heard this boy. He got up and he said, "I want to be president too and I want my wife to be first lady," and all that

stuff like that. And, you know, it just makes you want to get up and tell people the same way, and you feel the same way that they do.

A boy, less articulate, but with depth of feeling, said, "All I learned was that it's good to go down there and picket for your rights."

Perhaps the most important effect that the boycott movement had on the children was the hope it stirred that the future, because of their efforts, would not fulfill the promise of " . . . automated urbanity of 'nobodiness.' "[2]

BOY:

Well I think that we'd get somewhere . . . we wouldn't be left behind. And let the people know what we want and things like that—that we're not just nobody; we're somebody. We're human just like the rest . . .

We have seen that many of the boys and girls who emerged as leaders in the school boycott were themselves youngsters who had found the school experiences they had extremely threatening to themselves. Their senses of worth and dignity were constantly being threatened by attacks upon their self-concepts by teachers or by continual failure. Within the context of the civil-rights movement, these same boys and girls —the truants, the dropouts, the disruptive, and the actively hostile—were able to gain respect and pride in themselves. They had been asked to help; they were needed, wanted, and given active roles to play. The experience proved exhilarating to many. They were able to move from self-doubt to self-confidence. It was an experience of constructive growth and meaningful role development, as contrasted to the denigrating experiences of their school relationships, concerning which they spoke. They could now view their failures and difficulties, not in terms of personal inadequa-

[2] Sidney M. Wilhelm and Elwin H. Powell, "Who Needs the Negro?" *Trans-Action*, 1, Issue 6 (September-October 1964), 3-6.

cies, but rather as related to larger social issues like segregated schooling. They grew to understand that their problems were not peculiar to themselves but were shared by many within their social group. The solutions they sought were in the realm of social reality rather than in escapism by means of crime, drugs, or personal disintegration. Although they may not have learned algebra and French in freedom school, they did gain an increased awareness that education is important, and, even more, they learned respect for themselves.

11. CONCLUSION

THE SCHOOL SHUTDOWN called by Reverend Galamison and the Citywide Committee for Integrated Schools cannot be viewed apart from the larger Negro protest movement in America that seeks full equality for the Negro in American life and that views *de facto* school segregation as a main obstacle to that aim. Unlike many other protests or revolutions in history, this protest seeks to achieve goals and effectuate values that, as a nation, Americans have long professed to accept. As Daniel C. Thompson describes the movement:

> . . . Negro protest leaders do not advocate the overthrow of constitutional laws, changing the basic structure of our republican form of government, rearrangement of the American class structure, or the establishment of new political, economic, and ethical goals. Instead—except for a small extremist element—the Negro protest, itself, is a clear endorsement of the "American Creed" and a reaffirmation of the faith which the great majority of Negroes have in the

essential goodness of the individual and in the democratic process.[1]

Fundamentally, the school shutdown, although vigorously protesting the inadequacy of the school system, was asking that the schools implement a policy that was already official —the provision for "quality, integrated education." The leaders were asking that the plan recommended by the State Commissioner of Education be implemented. Thus, in the view of the leaders their action was not the illegal one, but rather they felt the school system had to respond to the legal requirements. For this reason, the legal strategy of the arrested boycotters was to seek the transfer of their court cases from family court and trial under the compulsory-attendance law to the Supreme Court and a hearing under the Civil Rights Act of 1964.

Tremendous changes have been occurring within the Negro protest movement over the last ten years. Perhaps the most significant of these has to do with the proliferation of Negro civil-rights organizations and the active personal involvement of thousands of people in militant action, often at great risk to their careers, their status, and their very lives. For most of this century, the civil-rights movement was in the hands of professionals like the staffs of the NAACP and the Urban League.[2] Within the last ten years, however, much of the initiative for change has come from militant individuals, outside the professional staff ranks, whose "segregation-bred frustration had been spilling over into action at an ever increasing rate."[3]

Earlier approaches, basically legal and educational, proved too slow at accomplishing "Freedom Now," that is,

[1] Daniel C. Thompson, "The Rise of the Negro Protest," *Annals of the American Academy of Political and Social Science*, 357 (January 1965), 20.
[2] James H. Laue, "The Changing Character of Negro Protest," *Annals of the American Academy of Political and Social Science*, 357 (January 1965), 120.
[3] *Ibid.*

true equality. Although Negroes have protested their lot for some 400 years, there has never been such large-scale mass participation in protest movements as has been the case since the Montgomery bus boycott of 1955-1956, when Dr. Martin Luther King, Jr., and his technique of nonviolent direct action rose to prominence.

Today, three types of Negro protest strategy dominate the American scene. Although these are not mutually exclusive techniques, the various organizations tend to emphasize one or the other. One approach, exemplified by the NAACP, is basically legal and seeks through the courts to end racial discrimination and segregation in American life. Another, educational, seeks to persuade and negotiate through means of research and information, exemplified by the Urban League and the Southern Regional Council. A third, activist, represented by CORE, the Southern Christian Leadership Conference, and the Student Nonviolent Co-ordinating Committee, seeks through direct confrontation with the supporters and tacit bystanders of segregation to appeal for change.[4]

These approaches are not mutually exclusive, and, indeed, pressures from militant members of Negro urban areas have forced many of the more moderate groups to take more activist positions in recent years. Reverend Galamison's group, the Citywide Committee for Integrated Education, is an activist group, prepared to take more militant action than were the larger civil-rights organizations in New York City at the time of the shutdown in question. Although he was not supported by the larger national organizations, it is important to note that he was not openly attacked by them.

The emphasis on self-help extends to all, including children. Participation of children in the New York City school boycotts was not an isolated phenomenon. Children have

4 *Ibid.,* pp. 121-125.

participated in almost every major recent civil-rights demonstration in this country. Their participation has been welcomed by civil-rights leaders. They appear to be less frightened, less discouraged, and ready for greater militancy than some of their elders. To the leaders and to the children themselves it seems essential that they take a part in the shaping of the future. Experience in the civil-rights movement provides opportunity for the socialization of the children for active roles in society.

The recent school shutdown came at a time when the national civil-rights organizations were devoting their energies to the development of increased political activity on the part of Negroes, especially concentrating on voter-registration drives and voter-education projects in the South. In New York City, the organizations were awaiting plans from the Board of Education, the latter having already made a formal commitment to search for means to improve education in the city for minority-group children. The Citywide Committee for Integrated Education considered that it had a role to play there. The shutdown was an extra warning that issues there had not really been resolved as yet, for the promise of change had not been fulfilled. In a sense, it provided the exclamation point to the protests that had gone before.

Conflicts like school boycotts may be said to be productive in several related ways other than those we have already discussed. Conflict leads to the modification and the creation of law; the application of new rules leads to the growth of institutional structures centering on the enforcement of these new rules and laws; and conflict brings into the conscious awareness of the contenders and the community at large norms and rules that were dormant before the particular conflict.[5] Let us turn to an examination of these points.

[5] Lewis Coser, *The Functions of Social Conflict* (New York: The Free Press, 1956), pp. 121-137.

Tremendous changes have occurred in American law and its judicial interpretation during the last ten years, from the national down to the local level. On the national level this struggle has culminated in the Civil Rights Act of 1964. On the local level, in New York, a shift away from the neighborhood-school concept has begun to take place. Thus in 1965, New York City lowered the grade level at which children could move to schools outside their neighborhoods.[6] These changes are related to this nation's shift from an agrarian to an industrial and technological society that increasingly rewards skills regardless of race and social origins. In such a society traditional segregation of the races and the newer *de facto* segregation of the cities that have helped maintain an unskilled lower class are no longer functional.

However, students of desegregation in this country have noted that virtually every case of desegregation in the United States has resulted from the need on the part of a community's leadership structure to resolve a crisis situation rapidly.[7] Many of these crisis situations have been the direct results of conflict—fear of loss of business due to demonstrations, fear of school closings, and the like. To the leaders of the school shutdown in New York, it seemed necessary to "keep things moving," to maintain a crisis situation, in order to make sure that the Board of Education would take action to resolve the educational problems of the city as defined by the protesters.

Second, we turn to an examination of the concept that an application of new rules leads to the growth of institutional structures centering on the enforcement of these new rules and laws. In this way, conflict, acting as a stimulus to

[6] The State of Massachusetts has passed a law denying state aid to schools with more than 50 per cent Negro enrollment. How this will affect the City of Boston, which maintains many *de facto* segregated schools, is still unclear.
[7] Laue, *op. cit.*, pp. 126-127.

change, makes possible the readjustment of relationships to changed conditions.[8]

Critics of the Negro civil-rights protests, and especially the school boycotts, have urged Negroes to stop demanding their rights and to devote their energies to utilizing these rights. It has been pointed out, however, in answer to these critics, that ". . . such advice ignores the growth potential of the protest itself. Negro Americans are learning how to be first class citizens at the same time they are winning first class citizenship."[9] We have seen that, in the course of the school shutdown, participants urged one another to consider their schooling seriously and sought to understand the impediments to their successful achievement within the school system. Thus their very protest was not a rejection of education but rather a turning toward it.

The required adjustment to changed social and political conditions is not confined to Negroes. School personnel, largely white, are learning that they too must readjust their traditional roles and functions to new conditions requiring truly equal educational opportunities for Negroes. The greatest difficulty faced by many educators may be the discomfort involved in facing up to the realization that the assumptions they had made concerning the equality of education provided in the city were not entirely valid. It has not been a simple matter for people who have thought of themselves as egalitarian in outlook and as dedicated to their work to recognize gross inadequacies in their traditional approach to children, parents, and other school personnel. Conflict has served then to require educators to examine their traditional approaches.

Although each school conflict, viewed superficially and in isolation, may appear to have been disruptive and negative

[8] Coser, op. cit., p. 128.
[9] Thomas F. Pettigrew, A Profile of the Negro American (Princeton: D. Van Nostrand Co., Inc., 1964), p. 167.

in effect, in actuality the conflicts were essential to the "shaking up" of existing structures and norms. American schools have been under stress from a population explosion, the vast proliferation of knowledge, and significant social and economic changes. Despite their efforts, educators in the past have not had the power to get adequate financial and moral support for significant improvement in the ability of American education to fulfill its goals of equal education for all according to their ability. The civil-rights movement, however, has helped to move concern for education to front-page news in America.

Viewed more specifically, Operation Shutdown in New York City can be seen as having performed several functions. It provided opportunity for those who were actively dissatisfied with the school experience to air their grievances. It united heterogeneous and dissident elements in a common protest. For example, juvenile gang leaders agreed to work together, suppressing intergroup disputes. The boycott served to focus public attention on the activity of the Board of Education and served notice concerning further potential protests and potential for violence if grievances were not answered. It served as constructive group protest, as opposed to individual protest born of frustration and pathology, which is more dangerous to self and perhaps to society. Last but not least, it increased confidence and practice in the art of social protest, as opposed to techniques of accommodation to inferior status previously practiced by Negroes in America, and gave the individual increased self-respect, a sense of importance, and opportunity to exert leadership.

Despite their heterogeneity, the participants in the boycott shared a common dissatisfaction with the experiences they had or were having in school, as well as an acute awareness of the subordinate position of Negroes in American life. These perceptions did not arise as a result of the boycott but preceded it, and the shutdown provided opportunity to express dissatisfaction with existing conditions.

Participation in the boycott was symptomatic of problems that had not been resolved. One of these problems is racial and class prejudice, which is perceived by these children as persisting in the schools and resulting in inferior education for Negroes. Related to this has been the failure of society adequately to provide through the schools or any other social agency constructive, nonpunitive efforts to help lower-class, minority-group children who experience academic or emotional difficulties in moving through the school system. A third series of problems revolves about the paucity of opportunity for young people to develop constructive roles and the urgent need to retain self-respect in school situations that are perceived as destructive.

Shortly after the shutdown ended, the "600" School Report was issued by the Board of Education, incorporating many recommended changes made by critics: Calvin Gross was dismissed as Superintendent of Schools; and a plan for implementation of the Allen Report was issued. Whether or not these events would have occurred anyway, in the same way and at the same time, is a moot question.

Adequate documentation of the general inferiority of public facilities made available for the education of lower-class youth has already been made. Today, two major forces are operating to change the picture. The civil-rights movement, on the one hand, is pressuring for schools that provide the kind of education that will give lower-status children the skills to enable them to function in upwardly mobile roles. The schools, too, are being pressured by larger economic and social forces that make large numbers of untutored, unskilled members of the population economically useless in urban life, as well as potentially dangerous socially.

We have explored some of the mechanisms by which the

schools are viewed by children as ensuring that the self-fulfilling prophecy of failure will work. Certainly if our goal is to provide the opportunity for all Americans, regardless of race or class, to operate on an economically and socially more constructive level made possible by our increasingly wealthy society, it behooves us to search for the impediments to that goal that the schools themselves have established. This is not to deny that family, community, and tradition play impeding roles also. But the fact that the school plays such a significant role has not been examined in adequate depth. Increased understanding of how the school environment is perceived by children is essential.

It would be sad indeed if more aid were poured into the schools with the same negative results because the subtle mechanisms for perpetuating status relationships remained unchanged. Where peer, family, and community support does not exist in enough strength to compensate for ineffective educational programs, serious reexamination of curriculum, methods, teacher attitudes, and general climate for learning must be made by urban school systems. Basically, the school must assume very seriously that its primary function is to teach rather than to contain.

BIBLIOGRAPHY

Ausubel, D., and Pearl Ausubel. "Ego Development Among Segregated Negro Children," in Harry A. Passow, *Education in Depressed Areas*. New York: Bureau of Publications, Teachers College, Columbia University, 1963.

Bank Street College of Education School and Mental Health Program, *Study of Social and Psychological Processes in the Classroom*, unpublished report.

Bartky, John A. *Social Issues in Public Education*. Boston: Houghton Mifflin Co., 1963.

Becker, Howard S. "Social Class Variations in the Teacher-Pupil Relationship," *Journal of Educational Sociology*, 25 (April 1952), 451–465.

———. "The Career of the Chicago Public School Teacher," *American Journal of Sociology*, 57 (March 1952), 470–477.

Better Education Through Integration. New York: The Board of Education, 1964.

In the Matter of Charlene Skipworth and Another. *14 Miscellaneous Reports*. 2nd Series, Albany, N. Y.: Williams Press, 1959, pp. 325–347.

Cicourel, Aaron V., and John I. Kitsuse. *The Educational Decision-Makers*. Indianapolis & New York: Bobbs-Merrill Company, Inc., 1965.

Clark, Kenneth B. *Dark Ghetto*. New York: Harper & Row, 1965.

———— and Mamie P. Clark. "Racial Identification and Preference in Negro Children," in Eleanor E. Maccoby, *et al.*, *Readings in Social Psychology*. New York: Holt, Rinehart & Winston, Inc., 1958, pp. 602–611.

Conant, James B. *Slums and Suburbs*. New York: McGraw-Hill Book Co., Inc., 1961.

Coser, Lewis. *The Functions of Social Conflict*. New York: The Free Press, 1956.

Davidson, Helen H., and Gerhard Lang. "Children's Perceptions of Their Teacher's Feelings Toward Them Related to Self-Perception, School Achievement and Behavior," *Journal of Experimental Education*, Vol. 29, No. 2 (December 1960).

Dentler, Robert A. "Dropouts, Automation, and the Cities," *Teachers College Record*, 65, No. 6 (March 1964), 475–483.

Desegregating the Public Schools of New York City, a report prepared for the Board of Education of the City of New York by the State Education Commissioner's Advisory Committee on Human Relations and Community Tension, 1964.

Deutsch, Martin. *Minority Groups and Class Status as Related to Social and Educational Factors in Scholastic Achievement*, Monograph No. 2, Society for Applied Anthropology.

Erikson, Eric Homburger. "The Problem of Ego Identity," *Journal of the American Psychoanalytic Association*, 5, No. 1 (1956), 58–121.

Goffman, Erving. "The Nature of Deference and Demeanor," *American Anthropologist*, 58 (June 1965), 473–502.

Grambs, Jean D. "The Self-Concept: Basis for Reeducation of Negro Youth," in William C. Kvaraceus, *et al.*, *Negro Self-Concept: Implications for School and Citizenship*. New York: McGraw-Hill Book Co., Inc., 1965, pp. 11–34.

Havighurst, Robert J. *The Public Schools of Chicago*. Chicago: The Board of Education, 1964.

Horney, Karen. *The Neurotic Personality of Our Time*. New York: W. W. Norton & Co., Inc., 1937.

Howe, Florence. "Mississippi's Freedom Schools: The Politics of Education," *Harvard Educational Review*, Vol. 35, No. 2 (Spring 1965).

Jaffe, Abram J., and Walter Adams. "Educational Attainment and Modern Technology," *Statistical News*, December 1964.

Jersild, Arthur J. *In Search of Self*. New York: Bureau of Publications, Teachers College, Columbia University, 1960.

Johnson, David W. *Changes in Self and Racial Attitudes of Negro Children Derived from Participation in a Freedom School*. New York: Institute of Urban Studies, Teachers College, Columbia University, 1964.

Kardiner, Abram, and Lionel Ovesey. *The Mark of Oppression: Explorations in the Personality of the American Negro*. Cleveland & New York: World Publishing Co., 1957.

Klineberg, Otto. "Negro-White Differences in Intelligence Test Performance: A New Look at an Old Problem," *American Psychologist*, Vol. 18, No. 4 (April 1963).

Kvaraceus, William C. "Negro Youth and Social Adaptation: The Role of the School as an Agent of Change," in Kvaraceus, *et al.*, *Negro Self Concept: Implications for School and Citizenship*. New York: McGraw-Hill Book Co., Inc., 1965, pp. 91–128.

Laue, James H. "The Changing Character of Negro Protest," *Annals of the American Academy of Political and Social Science*, 357 (January 1965), 119–126.

MacIver, Robert M. *The More Perfect Union*. New York: The Macmillan Co., 1948.

McKinney's Consolidated Laws of New York, Annotated, Book 16, Education Law. Brooklyn, N.Y.: Edward Thompson Co., 1953.

Mead, George Herbert. *Mind, Self, and Society.* Chicago: University of Chicago Press, 1934.

Merton, Robert K. *Social Theory and Social Structure,* rev. ed. New York: The Free Press, 1957.

Miller, Walter. "Implications of Lower Class Culture for Social Work," *Social Service Review,* Vol. 33, No. 3 (September 1959).

―――. "Lower Class Culture As a Generating Milieu of Gang Delinquency," *Journal of Social Issues,* Vol. 14, No. 3 (1958).

Moore, G. Alexander. *Urban School Days,* Project TRUE, Hunter College.

Myrdal, Gunnar. *An American Dilemma.* New York: Harper & Row, 1944.

New York Public Education Association. *The Status of Public School Education of Negro and Puerto Rican Children in New York City.* New York: 1955.

Peck, Sidney, and David Cohen. "The Social Context of *De Facto* School Segregation," *Western Reserve Law Review,* 16, No. 3 (May 1965), 572–607.

Pettigrew, Thomas F. "Negro-American Intelligence: A New Look at an Old Controversy," *Journal of Negro Education,* 33, No. 1 (Winter 1964), 6–25.

―――. *A Profile of the Negro American.* Princeton: D. Van Nostrand Co., Inc., 1964.

Plan for Integration. New York: The Board of Education, 1963.

Progress Toward Integration Sept. 1–Nov. 30, 1963 and Plans for the Immediate Future, interim report. New York: The Board of Education, 1963.

Segal, David. "Frustration in Adolescent Youth." U.S. Office of Education Bulletin, 1951.

Sexton, Patricia. *Education and Income.* New York: Viking Press, 1961.

Silberman, Charles E. *Crisis in Black and White.* New York: Random House, 1964.

Simmel, Georg. *Conflict,* trans. Kurt H. Wolff. New York: The Free Press, 1955.

————. *The Sociology of Georg Simmel,* trans. Kurt H. Wolff. New York: The Free Press, 1950.

"600" Schools, Yesterday, Today and Tomorrow. A Report to the Superintendent of Schools. New York: The Board of Education, 1965.

Sullivan, Harry Stack. *Conceptions of Modern Psychiatry.* Washington, D.C.: William Alanson White Psychiatric Foundation, 1947.

Taeuber, Karl E., and Alma F. Taeuber. *Negroes in Cities.* Chicago: Aldine Publishing Co., 1965.

Thompson, Daniel C. "The Rise of the Negro Protest," *Annals of the American Academy of Political and Social Science,* 357 (January 1965), 18–29.

Trillin, Calvin. "Letter from Berkeley," *New Yorker* (March 13, 1965), pp. 52–107.

Wilhelm, Sidney M., and Edwin H. Powell. "Who Needs the Negro?" *Trans-Action,* 1, Issue 6 (September-October 1964), 3–6.

Wolff, Max. *A Study of Racial Imbalance in the Plainfield Public Schools.* Plainfield, N.J.: The Board of Education, 1962.

Wilkerson, Doxey A. "Prevailing and Needed Emphasis in Research on the Education of Disadvantaged Children and Youth," *Journal of Negro Education* (Summer 1964), pp. 346–357.

Youth in the Ghetto. New York: Harlem Youth Opportunities Unlimited, Inc., 1964.